A Conversation
BETWEEN A BOY AND HIS DAD

A Conversation
BETWEEN A BOY AND HIS DAD

Simple Truths Hidden in Plain Sight

BY

PRISCO PANZA

ANGEL
EDITIONS

ISBN 978-1-7-335735-0-4

lifestyleconsultingservice.com

angeleditions.com

631.662.5310

805.699-6332

DEDICATION

To my Soul, for putting up with me for all these years

To my awesome parents, Rosemarie and Prisco

To my editor, Nancy Keller, who without her genius,
this book would not be available to you

And, last but not least, to every person
that has assisted me to get this far

Contents

Author's Note

An earnest conversation with my editor as the final draft of this book was being finished:

Nancy: Prisco, I want to talk to you about your use of bold in the text, and capitalization. You should get rid of the bold. If you feel that you must exaggerate a certain word, you can use italics. But ideally, you want to just have your words stand for themselves. Also, I understand why you are writing "response-ability" with a hyphen, but you are capitalizing it, and you are also capitalizing the word "soul." This is incorrect. These words should not be capitalized. I am going to change them. I just want to run it by you first.

Prisco: My dearest Nancy, I kindly appreciate your input and I value your expertise, as you have authored many books. However, as my mom would always say, I march to the beat of a different drummer. Throw out all the rule books, leave my bold alone, and keep your hands off my italics and capital letters. Period.

Nancy: Why would you want me to do that? If the reader is reading along and notices these things being incorrect, it will stop the flow of the thought.

Prisco: That's exactly what I want! You just made my

point! I **want** the reader to stop there! I want to get people to stop, and breathe, and notice, and think about these things, not just read along going to sleep! I want these things to stick in their minds, so that at some point, when life is happening and they are about to react to something, they will see it – **BAM!** – right in front of them – **Response-Ability**, in capital letters, and they will realize that they do have a choice.

Nancy: Oh, OK. Now I get it. Thank you for listening to my opinion, and now I do understand yours. You want me to leave all the bold, and the italics, and all the capital letters that you have written here?

Prisco: Yes! *That's why I wrote it like that!*

A Conversation
BETWEEN A BOY AND HIS DAD

By the way, you have your own play. It is your story, and your roadmap to your Divinity. All of humanity is and are the embodied master. You just hid the remembrance of it behind your story—which is the divine play, your life. It is the truth, yours and mine, hidden in plain sight.

I will share my story and how I unraveled it.

I notice that there seems to be a pattern to most of our human lives. An event, or series of events as in my case, that shuts us down. After this happens, we are usually asleep within the dream of our life. Then there is another event or series of events that does the opposite, wakes us up and reminds us that we are Divinity embodied. This is that story for me, and how it occurred between myself and my dad. My hope is that it will serve you and others in seeing the good and the light within yourself, and everything in life, if that is your choice.

My Story

THIS IS THE STORY of a boy and his becoming a man, not only in the physical sense but in the spiritual sense as well. Metaphorically the title stands for many things and has many meanings, for myself as well as for all who will read this story.

My dad and I didn't really talk that much, so often I did not know what he was thinking and feeling, or why. Therefore, this story is mostly about the dialog in the six inches between my ears. As of late my dad and I do have deeper meaningful conversations, and a far better understanding of one another, and that sure is nice.

Choice determines destiny. But what determines your choices? And how and when do we start making these choices? As I share my story you will see how my choices and decisions about my circumstances, people, places, and things shaped my life. You will see how my formed opinions and judgments created my perceptions, or I should say, misperceptions. In doing so, I will take you on a journey into my play, aka story, that may feel keenly familiar and may shed some light on some questions you may have about yourself.

This is my story. I'm choosing to tell it, and as I share it, I am releasing it in every aspect of my being and in all of my lineage that carried this story for all the eons that have passed.

My story kept me trapped in my dream, in that endless loop of doing and mediocrity that is most of our lives. You might even know it well. Basically most stories look like this: Somehow get up each day, go to school and/or work, come home, take care of whatever responsibilities you have – homework, the dog, the kids, dinner, etc. – and do this all as fast as you can so you can watch your favorite TV show, then go to bed, somehow sustain your relationship, and ponder, what the heck just happened? What am I doing here? Is this all there is to life? And the next day, get up and do it all over again, and again, and again.

No, this is not everyone's story, but it was mine. It was this story that I held onto for dear life, and it was the story that allowed me to stay asleep within the dream and create my most magnificent, distorted misunderstanding of love and my life. It stemmed from a misunderstanding of my father's love, which in my case includes both of my parents as well as Creator, my Divine Father. However, my anger was directed mostly at my dad, not so much at my mom or Creator. I made my dad my fall guy, the proverbial scapegoat. He was and still is the lead character in my play. I realize now how strong he had to be to play that part, and I am grateful for it, for him, for all he does, all he did, and even for the way it was done

This anger at the Male, including myself, came from many sources, the first of which was a distortion of my perceptions by my belief in original separation from Source, Creator, Divinity, God, or whatever that is for you. From there it splintered down through the eons of time in my many variations and incarnations. This allowed me to feel *insignificant, less than, not enough,* and *not loved.* This "not loved" perception was the underpinning of the story of my life, and it allowed me to feel and experience separation as being real in my life. It kept me longing for my dad's approval and endlessly searching outside of myself for some validation or meaning for my existence. It allowed me to create a life of illusion that I was not enough, not good enough – and heck, I was never going to be enough, either.

You see, for me, in the beginning, Creator, God, Source was neither male nor female. At the very least, for me it was a combination of all energies in this dance of oneness. Creator, with its amazing sense of humor, created me as it did all of us, as an aspect of itself, to allow it to have fun and experience the ALL in a way it hadn't before. And so, after much deliberation and conversation, down the hatch I went, into the experience of perceived separation and not remembering who I was, where I came from, or what I was doing here. It is safe to say that, at the very least, I don't think I was very crazy about this idea of separating from the comforts of home and coming here to have this experience, or so it felt.

Now, I know what caused me to come here, why I came, and why I am here. But that's a story for another time.

I know that when I first arrived here I was a clean sponge, ready to absorb all that was to be offered. I could communicate quite well, but only through telepathy, as we all could. Right from the start my parents were at a distinct disadvantage, as most parents are. (As the adults they are, most parents gave up this form of communication early in their lives. I will explain more on this later.) So these totally new parents were going to raise another being that they had produced, with no prior experience, no help, be responsible for it, and I didn't even have the courtesy to come with an instructions manual or speak a language that they could relate to. Basically they were in for it. I don't know about you, but to me, I think having a child has got to be the most exhilarating and scary prospect that life can offer. Right there, this explains a lot for me, as this is where all the miscommunication and misunderstanding began for this lifetime.

Eventually I gave up trying to communicate and went into the usual learning process and learned to communicate their way, forgetting about telepathy. There is great significance in that "gave up trying" statement. It was a foretelling of how I was going to be for the rest of my physical life until now, when I finally woke from the dream, opened up and embodied my awareness and wisdom. This is what every experience in my life was trying to do, to open me up to this. Only I did not see this then.

There was something powerful in that "giving up," as this was one of the first times that I gave away my power to that which was outside of myself, and began to close down.

2

My Life

A S A YOUNG BOY growing up in Port Jefferson, New York, I would often play in our large front yard. Being outside and having fun was the best part of life back then. Playing in the dirt, climbing trees, riding my bike, drinking from the garden hose, creating a fort from the giant cardboard box a washing machine was delivered in at the neighbors' house, and hanging out with my friends. It was like you could escape everything, and anything that you didn't understand or that hurt you. It felt as if nothing mattered anymore and like nothing could touch you out there. I always felt different from others and felt like I didn't quite fit in. A bit of an oddball if you will, and as I remember it, I spent a fair amount of time alone.

I loved the summers as a kid. In the summer I would lie on the warm, soft green grass, letting the gentle summer breeze just caress my face. I would

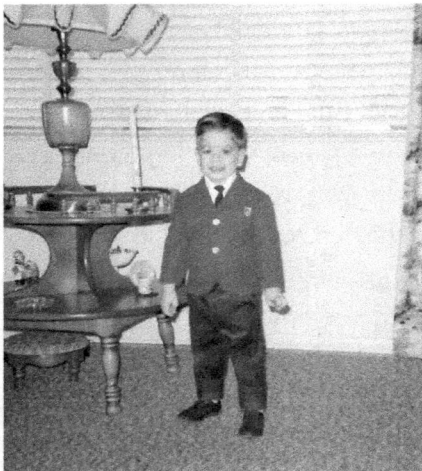

This is a picture of me when I was somewhere around 3 or 4 years old, in our living room in our Port Jefferson, New York home, circa 1968 or 1969.

gaze up at the sky, looking up between the sparkling green oak trees at the beautiful blue canvas above. I would let my imagination run wild with all kinds of dreams, many of which have come to pass. In the fall, as I would lie there in the cool green grass, it was thicker and softer than usual, because my dad would always fertilize and seed then. I loved raking leaves into a pile and diving in. Yes, I said rake – there were no leaf blowers at my house, and man, we had leaves.

There was a neighborhood in a different section of town where the policy was to rake all the leaves to the curb and then the town came by and picked them up. I loved riding my bike through them as fast as I could. These piles were as long as the streets, and four to six feet high in some places. Lucky for me, this development was hilly. I would gather as much speed as my legs could give me and ride my bike through the leaves at breakneck speed. Of course this led to the occasional crash, but hey, that's what guardian angels are for. They were always on high alert and working overtime with me.

Lying in the leaves in the fall was another favorite thing to do. I loved the way they smelled. I would lie there and just breathe. It was then that I would see the amazing color show before my eyes. I used to lie in wonder at how a little acorn knew how to grow into this mighty oak that I was lying under and/or climbing. How the trees and leaves knew when and how to change into the most magnificent of colors. Only an infinite imagination could create this, I would muse to myself. Little did I realize that this same Imagination created me, too, and kept every bodily function in perfect harmony at every moment of every day.

My eyes occasionally caught a passing puffy snow white cloud, and I would allow my imagination to see what it could create from that puffy white cotton ball in the sky. Funny thing what happened – often, as I noticed what I was thinking, what might be in the cloud, what it might look like, it began to take the shape of that thing. I just knew there was something to that. I believed even back then that I could create shapes with the clouds.

In the winter months I would go sledding with friends on our Flexible Flyers, toboggans, and on anything else that would slide. We would go to any big hill or any sump that still had snow, have snowball fights, and go skitching (as we called it) behind random cars – and how we prayed for a truck!

What is skitching, you ask? Skitching is crouching into a squat position behind a car or truck and letting it pull you in the snow while you hang onto the bumper. Of course the drivers never suspected a thing. OK, so there was this one time we spied this guy as the perfect target. What is a perfect target? A four wheel drive truck. We all jumped on and I was crouching down behind the truck, as this all had to be perfectly timed and done so the driver did not see you doing it. Well, he did, as I saw his face in the rear view mirror through the pickup's back window, and I just knew. Normally we might go an eighth to a quarter of a mile or so, as they would have to stop at the stop signs on the street and we would drop off. He didn't stop at any, so after what seemed like a mile or so of this craziness we just all decided to tuck and roll and hope for the best. I had to give my guardian angels something to do, right?

When I was younger and much wiser, I stayed closer to home. I would get dressed up in a snowsuit, boots, hat, scarf and gloves, and my younger brother and I would build snow tunnels and igloos in the massive snowdrifts and in the piles of plowed snow by the curbs. It was always so peaceful, quiet and warm in there. I would lay in there for hours, just allowing my imagination to take me away. I would often say to myself as I looked skyward through a tunneled skylight, I know I am not from here, but I am here, and I am so confused.

I felt so separated and isolated in a world I didn't know or understand, and no one was explaining it to me in a way I could understand. I would be told things by my parents, but not explained to. I felt as if there was no place to go to ask questions or to get answers, and I sure did not have it within me to go within, as I was never taught or had the example of doing so, that I remember. (Although there was, for a time, when my mom and dad were practicing Transcendental Meditation when I was young. It was quite popular back in the 70s. I'm not really sure what ever happened with that.)

So, of course, the journey of too many moments to count began, of looking outside of myself. For, surely, there must be an answer for me, somewhere out there. It seemed as if I was often trying to have some other experience, something other than the one I was having at that moment, looking outside of myself for some other something. I was rarely satisfied in the moment, and let's face it, I definitely was not present in the now. And so, I looked in all the usual places. I looked to the church which my family attended and relied on, especially in the tough times.

My extended family was a big influence, too – my Aunt Betty, Uncle Henry, and my cousins Prisco (yup, there is another one), Happy, Phyllis, Joey, and also my grandparents. They all lived in the same home, what to me was a house larger than life and filled with this special love that there are no words for. How I loved and still love them dearly. It was my second family. We shared so much, and their influence ran deep in me.

So I did my best to be a good Catholic, as that was my family's religion and, well, it seemed to be working for them. Or so I thought at the time.

It seemed that my parents thought the priests, pastors and reverends had it right and had all the answers. But to me that always felt just a bit off, and at times even turned my stomach, especially when you had to recite certain scriptures or doctrine. There was this one time, I remember sitting there saying to myself, really, you didn't just say that, it doesn't even make sense. Eeeeeek!

Then there were my teachers. Surely they must know something, as they were teachers, right? I was a sensitive kid, and learning for me was an emotional experience to say the least, so nothing ever seemed to sink in. Most of what they had to say went over my head and I always had this "less than" feeling as I struggled to learn at the same pace as the other kids. Eventually I gave up on myself (here is the supporting theme again), as I assumed that my teachers didn't care. I felt so insignificant, as I had no idea what I wanted to do with my life. It seemed everyone else just played follow the leader and somehow knew. (Although, fast forward to today, I've come to realize that a lot of them changed majors, schools, careers, wives, well you get the point.)

I distinctly remember this one time when I felt totally broken, in spirit mostly, but physically as well. I was in seventh grade at JFK Junior High and it was the final for my math class. It was almost summer on Long Island then, and it was hot that June day, with no air conditioning in school. (And let's not forget, five miles uphill – oh, sorry, I digress, that's a different story.) There I was in the middle of this test, and I just choked up. I don't remember if it was a final or a state regents test, which is just another test you could take if you wanted that degree/diploma also. I just choked up. I couldn't get my brain to function to figure out the answers or remember anything. The fear and frustration got so great, I just gave up. Gave up right there. Quit, closed the test, and walked out. Every negative thought that little voice could come up with, it did. It was a concerto of cuss words. I remember my head reeling with confusion about what might happen. My imagination – you know, the little voice – went into overdrive. I'm no good, nothing I ever do is right, I'm never good enough. What would my grade be? Would I have to go to the dreaded summer school? What would the teacher say? And then the biggie – what would my parents say, especially my dad? To say the least, I felt like I had let them all down and that I was just some loser.

(Yet somehow I received a regents diploma in high school – go figure, right? I even scored a 1320 out of 1600 on my SAT's. I don't say this to brag, but to set a point for later in the book regarding where my focus is, and recognizing my own worth.) That day hurt so much, but it wasn't until I got older that I realized that the only person that felt let down and hurt that day was me. How could this have affected anyone else, when I never told anyone until now? So the only one that *could* be affected was me.

My main guides in my life were and still are my mom and dad. Don't get me wrong, they were great examples in many ways, but I never had the wisdom as a young boy to see it, let alone understand or comprehend it. I didn't realize until much later on that there is a world of difference between being talked *to,* or talked *with,* and being talked *at.* At the time, it just felt to me like I was not getting the love that I needed, in the way that I needed it. And, by the way, *No One Ever Said They Didn't Love Me.* I assumed from how I felt that this was so. Boy, did this assumption create a life!

And so it began. I built a world around myself in which I truly believed that I was not good enough, and that no one cared about me or loved me. Sometimes I wasn't even sure if I was seen, let alone heard. No matter where I looked, there was the same *no one cares,* reinforcing my feeling of *less than* and *not good enough.* I created this in my life right down to a religion that says that if you don't do this the right way, you're *less than.* I don't say this lightly, as now I realize those early misperceptions helped me to create my opinions and judgments, and these were the glue that held my story together and formed my belief systems. And all along I kept saying the same statement: I know I am not from here. As time went on, I began to follow that with: I must be from somewhere, but where?

3

In the Beginning

OF COURSE I AM NOW telling this story from a hindsight perspective, so let's start at the beginning.

There I was, in all my Realized Divinity in, well, we'll just use the word Heaven, with Creator, and my mom and dad, who I picked for this go round. I chose them as the perfect Souls to assist me in this journey to awaken to my Divinity while still in my humanity.

So there we are, all of us – Creator, myself, and my mom and dad – all having one last conversation before I head down the hatch. I realize now that this one last conversation was the review of The Greatest Play Ever Written, my divine plan, my whole life plan, the whole enchilada. Dammit man, I knew I should have paid closer attention while the Big Guy was reviewing the play that *we* (Creator and I) wrote for *me*. In the moments before leaving, I knew

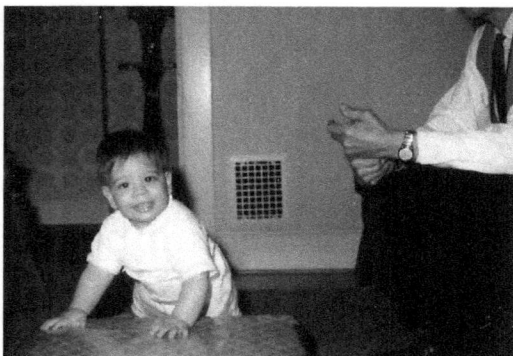

This is a picture of me when I was somewhere between 18 months to 2 years old, in my dad's parents' house in West Haven, Connecticut, circa 1966 or 1967. The man to the right of me is my grandfather. He was, and still is, very close to me.

I was shutting down and getting emotionally charged, so I quit, I shut down. (Note what I said about shutting down in the last two paragraphs of Chapter 1, and in the fourth paragraph from the end of Chapter 2. Don't be lazy, go back and read it!) In that moment with Creator, and my mom and dad, I didn't hear what I needed to remember to make this journey not quite so painful. Oh, I was listening, but all I remember was Blah, Blah, Blah, Blah. Little did I know that this was the secret code! But, the big BUT here is, it set a pattern for the lifetime that I (and many of us) deal with every day. You ask, what pattern is that? It's the *I am not loved* and/or *not good enough, never enough, I gave up on me* one.

Boom! So down the hatch I go. OK, here I am on earth, as a baby on my way out—and by the way, as I stated earlier, I don't speak their language and I left the playbook up there, so my parents are distinctly at a disadvantage. First thing the Doc said was, there is no manual attached, good luck with this one. I can only imagine how excited and scared my parents must have been. The flood of human emotions, from relief to joy to outright fear, should about sum it up, especially as I was their first child. After I was born I imagine their first words aloud to be how cute I was – but to themselves they probably muttered, *now* what do we do?

Choice Determines Destiny

DESTINY IS DETERMINED by choice, your choice. Consciously or not, only you can know for sure, for you. Life is not some hand dealt to you. You Created It All. And either you accept 100% *full* responsibility for your life and take your power back so you can begin to re-create your life through a different awareness, or you put your power outside yourself, in something or somebody else, God, or otherwise. It's your call. And when I speak of power I mean Blame, especially in regard to Creator or God. Nowadays I am well aware of how and why Creator's Cosmic Conscious Energy is what sustains me, but I was not aware of this back then, even though I have always been the one creating with that energy. Earlier in my life, I put my power outside of myself, and in so doing, I created a lot of suffering for myself and others. As a child I perceived my life to be painful, and I believed that my parents did not love me, especially my dad. As I said earlier, he was elected, *by me,* to be the fall guy that I would scapegoat in my younger years as the bad guy.

I am not going to bash my parents with examples of my perceived misunderstandings. That serves no one. I will, however, tell you that at times we fought like cats and dogs, went together like oil and water. But by no means was it all bad.

I had gotten so good at this game of misperception that there was a period of time in my life that I thought of taking my own life because the pain I had created within was so great.

And then there was the fateful day. I remember it vividly. I was about 14 or 15, and it was a warm but clear summer day. At the time I used to mow different lawns in the neighborhood, and sometimes take care of the neighbors' house when they would travel in summer. It was already late in the afternoon and the day was beginning to cool down. I could smell the fragrance of fresh cut grass, a favorite of mine, as I had finished our lawn and theirs.

I was standing in my neighbors' driveway, straddling my red Huffy 10-speed bike after finishing some chores at the house, and I was about to take off to go to the Police Athletic League where I had been boxing for some years already, when it hit me. Hey! I have choices. Three to be exact.

One: I could check out of here. It certainly seemed reasonable enough, given how I felt, and I could even write a note so everyone would know how I felt so there was no confusion. Riiiiiiiight. Two: I could check my dad out. Yup, I said it. I thought about that. But also I realized that for every choice there is an equal reaction or consequence, and I was not willing to bear that on any level. Three: and here we go, my final shutdown to my Divinity – I just closed myself off to feeling anything, and I do mean anything.

(I had experienced another shutdown earlier in my life, but it was partial, and wouldn't you know, at that time, all of a sudden I'd needed glasses. Hmmm – think there is a correlation?)

And so now with my Divinity fully hidden in my story of *no one loves me*, *never enough* and *I am not enough*, I couldn't live out my life's play that I had written earlier – or so I thought.

Maybe, just maybe, this *is* the play, the life script, destiny, theme, the issue to be resolved in this lifetime. It sure is beginning to look like it, to me. I came to realize much later in life that there were many variations or re-writes that could have taken place that would have been less painful. (However, lessons learned make for great examples for others to learn from, pointing the way for them to do just the opposite – hint, hint.) And so for the next sixteen years or so I was in this feeling coma, creating a life of feeling *not loved, less than, not enough*, and *never enough*.

Life feels surreal as I look back in reflection on the decisions of my life, especially one of my biggest decisions: my relationship with my first wife. I now see why I made the choices I did, from that *less than, never enough,* and *not loved* energy of my story. And this was the version of my play that I picked till the next big event in my life: my first marriage ending.

5

Wake-up Call Number One

IT WAS THE DISSOLUTION of my first marriage in my thirty-first year of life that triggered a major wake-up call to shake me out of my slumber. It did so by causing me to look really closely at why I felt like such a failure. I was so down and disappointed in myself. I had to begin, at the very least, to look at my feeling of *not good enough* or *not enough,* and the accompanying despair and utter disappointment in myself which were the flavor of the day as far as feelings that were coming up for me at that moment.

I remember lying on my couch one day with my Bible on my chest just trying to get close to something that I believed was so far outside of me. (And by the way, here is a good example of how I was thinking and how far outside of myself I was looking, as the Catholic doctrine I had been exposed to taught that God is somewhere out there, not within me, or part of me.) I remember feeling so much internal pain that my chest physically hurt, my heart actually ached. It was a day like any other, only on this day I lay paralyzed in my own fear, looking upward out the window at the blue and gray autumn sky. The maple trees were already a deep yellow, and they were just starting to drop their leaves. I remember lying there watching the gentle breeze move the branches from side to side and the leaves floating gently to the ground. It was as if gravity didn't quite have a hold on them. I remember thinking to myself, there must be more to this life than pain.

As I began to seek answers, the teachers showed up, one by one, in their due time. The next twenty-two years would be a remarkable ride back to my realization that I already *am* my Divinity realized. I just had to recognize, claim and fully embody it. Only I had no idea of that then, let alone what that actually meant. I still thought there was something I had to do to earn or become it.

And so for the next twenty-two years a myriad of individuals came and went from my life, and still do, to this day. They came to teach, to guide, to support, and still others to protect. They came in the form of coaches, friends, family, teachers, healers, doctors and, well, you get the idea. The common theme that they all had was a deep love of themselves. Each in their own way, they shared that with me, allowing me, in my own way and time, to open up to the idea of something different than what I was thinking and believing about myself and my life.

The next big wake-up call was when I met my second wife, and the life we shared together for seventeen of those twenty-two years. It was there, in the many relationships that were born in that span of time, that real growth was happening. Sometimes I knew it and other times I didn't. At the times when I knew it, I was able to flow with whatever was happening at the time and learn easily from it. At other times I did not see it so easily and resisted, and in so doing caused myself and others quite a bit of discomfort, heartache and pain.

It was after that marriage ended that I was able to really examine my own energy and how my many perceptions, opinions, judgments and beliefs had formed my life, my story, my play of life. It was then that I had many eye-opening moments – one of which was taking 100% responsibility for my life in all areas, not just the ones I thought were mine or that I felt comfortable with.

Believe me, when you do this, the opposition is staunch from a variety of sources, as this is the key to dismantling your story's cornerstone belief that people, places and things outside of yourself cause you to be or to feel a certain way. One that I never saw coming was from some of my associations with individuals in, well, we will just call it my spiritual community. There were those who would say things like, "You have every right to be hurt and feel like you do," or "XYZ was not good," or "XYZ was totally wrong." Note the opinion/judgment here, allowing me to hold my story if I so chose. **There is always an opportunity for choice. (Warning!!! There will always be these decisive key moments for you to make a decision. Hint hint.)**

I would say to them, "Who cares about that, I am not interested in being Right, I am interested in being my brightest Light, and sharing it." They would project onto me *their* fears of letting go of *my* story, because if I was even remotely on the higher path, they would surely have to let go as well, and obviously they were not ready. Other people will try to keep you in character in your story, your play. This is why it is so important to choose wisely when you are picking a mate, friends, job, career, mentor, coach, etc.

The funny thing about energy is that if while observing life (energy) as it passes through you,

you have judgments or opinions on those observations, you hold the energy bound around those issues, and therefore you hold everything bound at that level of frequency, whether it is a hurt, or a wound, or anything else. This is where I experienced my *lack* and/or *less than* life from. I have often said that opinion/judgment is the glue that holds your story together, it is the binding agent.

If you want 100% of what life has to offer, you have to play at 100% on all levels, not just the ones you want. I am not saying you can't pick and choose what to deal with and when, but that it's better to do it on your own terms, not when life throws you a curve ball like a disease or somebody you cherish passing away when you're not expecting it. We all put things and conversations off for as long as we can due to fear, only to have them explode on us at the most inopportune times.

Life has a way of showing up in our relationships, places, things, pets, finances, wherever you're willing to look. Not even Creator is free from pain, suffering or anything we deem negative, for if it was, Creator would be void of something, and that's not possible, as Creator is everywhere, all things and void of no-thing.

And as Creator is all things, thus Creator experiences all of it, just without judgment or opinion, allowing the great ebb and flow of Life rather than the resistance of opinion and judgment. Therefore Creator experiences it but has a whole different experience around it, as Creator's perception is, it is all good.

6

I Can't or I Won't

AM I STUCK IN my story because I can't, or because I won't, do something about it? And can I actually do something to change it? Yes – however, there were plenty of days, and still are sometimes, that I didn't and don't feel that way. I am not saying that I am some self-proclaimed master of life and energy. I am just like you, a human with everyday human experiences, remembering why I came here. And that is to remember that I Am and you are, we all are, our Divinity already embodied. We just hide it really well.

As I began to answer this question as honestly as I could, I realized how statements like *I can't, I don't know, whatever, I don't care, what's the difference, it doesn't matter, who cares* – these statements or words come from a place of lack and disempowerment. I had uttered these statements every day in my life with no knowledge of their power. (In a later chapter I will talk briefly about the power of the spoken word.) This came from my learned perceptions, as I observed my life through my opinions and judgments.

Perception itself, along with the often unrecognized story we attach to it, creates an imaginary relationship between people, places and things. In my life the bridge came from putting my power outside of myself, usually through placing blame and/or responsibility onto others or self, to connect my story line to my physical life. Without my opinions or judgments of good or bad, right or wrong, I would have no play, and this dream I was living would be over. I would be living my version of heaven on earth, which I am now. I am not saying it's all peaches and cream, I just do not judge it as much, and I am very careful around opinions, so things don't stick around so long.

For example, this statement: *Life is good*. In reality, life is life and good is good. They are not connected until you use your perception and judgment to connect them with *is*. Then you proceed to feel a certain way, usually based on some opinion or judgment of someone or something that is occurring or has occurred. It's the same for this example: *Life is bad*. In reality, life is life and bad is bad. It isn't until we connect them with that itsy bitsy word *is*, in our perceptions creating expectations, that we cause ourselves pain.

Let's use me as an example, as I love to do. So the story goes, I asked her out and for her number and she said yes. OK, so I'm on a roll, life is good, I'm feeling great. I send her a text later that day and she replies, "I did not want to be rude and not exchange numbers, but I am actually in a committed relationship." Vexed expectations are surely a cause of pain.

Wait! What or who just pulled the carpet out from under my feet? I did, since I gave my power away to the experience that just occurred. I did not have to, I had a choice, which I quickly made later. I took full responsibility for my actions in what my Soul was asking me to see, and it had a beneficial outcome and effect on me. Before asking her, I had heard clearly: leave the situation alone. But my ego got the better of me. And so I proceeded, and well, I learned a valuable lesson about how if you say something to your Soul about giving yourself over to it, that means all of you and all things, including girls. I will go into this later in the chapter on Response-Ability, as this is how I choose to create my life now.

A deeper example is: *I Am Prisco*. Here we are connecting I and Prisco. I Am is I Am, or to really simplify it, I is I and Prisco is Prisco. They are not connected until we assume they are, and we say they are united as one by using the verbiage at hand. As I is I and Prisco is Prisco they are interchangeable, and if only one was left, I would still be here, as I or as the human (let's say Prisco), but I would still always just be. This is why the I Am statements are so powerful, as I Am means to say in layman's terms, I'm here, I exist, and/or I create. For those more advanced on your journey, yes there is more to this, but for the sake of keeping it simple I will not be going into how I Am is equal to AUM (OM) and what that vibration really means. As my mom would say, think before you speak. I have taken that wisdom to myself and compassionately reminded myself to breathe before I speak.

The perceptions, opinions and judgments we learn are what create our world of separation. It is the dream that Oneness has to have in order to play this game we call Life. Without this dream, our play, we could not have this separation experience. The ultimate question here is: Do you want to be awake within the dream? If so, keep reading.

Let us first discuss perception. Perception is a bridge, the imaginary relationship between things, people, places and/or events. Some say that what we perceive is because of the "veil" that hides our truth from us. Well let's talk about this so-called

veil, and how it hides our truth. We should understand this thing that so many speak of.

The truth is that there is no veil, there is only
perception, which we are taught through our experiences with our teachers, preachers and family (TP&F). It is in this ignorance that we become
veiled to the truth. I am not so sure I buy the no-
tion that we came here with no knowledge of our
Divinity. I am confident that we have full recollec-
tion upon first arriving as a newborn, but soon,
through outside influence, we come to believe
otherwise. So it's sort of a game of the blind leading the clean slate, and the little sponges we are
can't communicate in a way most understand, because it's telepathic, as I said earlier. And so we just
allowed our TP&F to lead the way, as they never
seemed to come around to our way of being. Of
course this does not happen without a fight from
our little beings. It's like I stated earlier, I knew I
was in this world, but not of it. Which I believe
is where all of my rebellion came from. A quote
from Abraham-Hicks sums it up quite well:

"The children desire freedom! And every par-
ticle of their being from their Source says, 'You are
free. You are so free, that every thought you offer,
the entire Universe jumps to respond to it.' And
so, to take that kind of knowledge and try to con-

fine it in any way, defies the Laws of the Universe. You must allow your children to be free, because the entire Universe is set up to accommodate that. And anything you do to the contrary will only bring you regret. You cannot contain those that cannot be contained. It defies Law."

My words: The human physical body is a containment vessel, which is why it has an expiration date and you die. Your Soul cannot be contained, nor does it wish to be. However, to my understanding, it is willing to stay much longer in this vessel if you will expand yourself to embody it within the very fabric of all of your being, communing with it daily. This will require you to gain an expansive outlook on yourself and on life.

OK, back to the topic at hand. Why do I say "imaginary bridge"? Well it has to be imaginary, and it has to be your imagination, not someone else's. Oh yes, you learned to do it, or took it on, but you did it. So if you can imagine it one way, you can certainly imagine it another. How do I know? Because I came to realize that everything I perceived and believed was a choice of my own focus. I had to admit this in order to be able to take 100% responsibility for my life, in order to re-create it. If it were not so, you would be powerless to change, and that, my friend, couldn't be further from the truth. Oh, it or you may at times feel that way, as I said I have my own days, but I assure you, you are far from powerless. So this is not a story about taking or finding your or my power, but a remembering that you've had it all along. And to top it off, it was hidden in plain sight.

I will never forget the day that I realized this intellectually. Not embodied it, but first saw this. I laughed so hard at myself and said, You bleepity bleep, no one hid it from you, you hid it from yourself, to play this game!

I finally realized that it wasn't that I couldn't change, but that I wouldn't, because of my own lack of self-awareness. I realized that this was because I was not awake in my observation of myself. I still had opinions and judgments about myself. In the instant that I became aware or awake in the dream of perception, I was empowered to change anything and everything I chose, through making a different choice. And thus a new Response-Ability was born.

Now getting this intellectually and embodying it are far from the same.

Herein lies the key: It already was embodied in me. It always was in every cell, fiber and atom of my being. It is in everyone and everything; it is the very fabric of life. I just had to allow it, and what that really means is, stop denying that I am the creator of my own life and that I also embody Creator itself. I had to learn/remember how to accept/allow/receive this as it already was – but the beliefs I had taken on about myself were the opposite of this. I had to *just let it be*. I had to put aside the definitions and boundaries that I had taken on.

So my first question was: What if, for just one minute, just a brief moment, I were to put aside judgments, opinions, boundaries and definitions in my life? And what if I were to just try it out to see what observing myself without opinions or judgments would look, feel, smell, sound and taste like? **I mention the senses because they are our main entry points to opinion and judgment.**

As I did this, I realized that there was no one and no thing – nothing – defining or limiting my life. Not even myself anymore, as I was the only one who could. No one, no thing, nothing asking me to defend my life, insisting that it be a certain way, or demanding that I resolve anything. The funny thing was, I could still hear, see, feel, taste, touch, smell, think, imagine, and choose. But the difference was, I did not decide who or what was doing it, not even myself. This was my first real experience of *just being*.

Getting Unstuck

GETTING UNSTUCK was now a somewhat simple concept for me to see, but it was not so easy for me to embody. The solution, for me, was to in a sense separate cause and effect. This was not so simple for me, as I'd had a lifetime of programming to believe that people, places, circumstances and/or things outside of myself had caused my life to be the way it was. It is a bit of a leap to realize that life happens *through* you, not *to* you. This, however, is one of the many Universal Laws: We are free beings. It can only be this way, and with my permission, as this is what I agreed to with Creator before I embarked on this journey, and it is with my perception that I see it this way, or not. If this was not true then I would not have the power to change my life, and I do, so this proves it for me.

I always take it back to myself. I look for concrete proof from my results in my life. For you to do this requires you to observe yourself, preferably from a neutral place, letting your conscience be your guide.

Here are some observation examples.

This is an example of an opinion or judgment statement: I am a really poor soccer player. Here is the same statement as an example of neutral observation: I have not scored a goal in 20 games. It's simply not critical.

Example 2: That is a gorgeous man walking down the street. A more neutral way of seeing and stating it would be, there is a person walking. Now this will take some getting used to, as your ego will say really, do we need to be that dull, blah, etc.?

It's your choice. Allow your Soul to guide you, or do as you wish. I'm just conveying what I did. I said to my ego, if you keep it up I will duct tape you shut so you can't speak your opinions or judgments. Just kidding – but all joking aside, we had many compassionate heart-to-heart conversations about this daily, and still do. Oh, and here is a friendly reminder – this is not, nor is life, a destination game. I don't believe that exists. I just do my best to have as much compassion as I can for myself all day every day. One benefit of this is that I am compassionate to everyone else, as well. If you observe yourself in opinion and/or judgment, be gentle with yourself and just say, OK, how could I reframe it, and do so.

Hint: You will do this often. Who cares? The fact that you're even aware is a home run.

It has been (sometimes brutally) brought to my attention that my ego will struggle with this concept of awakening itself because it has taken the stance (perception) that it, me, we, need to do something to deserve awakening to this new way of observing me. Also remember that the ego's stance is one of protector. It will feel threatened and think that it's being overthrown. I have witnessed it become so strong that individuals think it is actually someone else holding them back. This is the point of the many compassionate conversations, to reassure it. At any rate, I was left with this observation: As I learn to observe less critically, starting with myself and my life and then moving on to observe others less critically and with less opinion and/or judgment, my experience of life is altered.

As I got to this point in my experiences I found that my deepest wisdom was beginning to strongly confront my conditioned perceptual upbringing. Some refer to this as the dark nights of the Soul. Notice I said nights, plural, as this is a process to clear this from your system. It's not that you take some weekend course and you're clear of your perceived wounds. You will only resist what your nervous system is not prepared to receive. All things must be processed through both nervous systems, etheric and physical. If it all cleared at once, your physical body would not be up for that all at one time. Good God, man, give yourself at least a month of weekend classes and then you will know the master within. OK, I jest here, but my point is, be kind to yourself in this process.

This is what I discovered for *myself*. My feelings are real. I am really feeling this. My thoughts are real. I am really thinking this. However, my thoughts don't cause my feelings. My circumstances are real. I am really experiencing this. However, my circumstances don't cause my feelings. My learned perceptions, judgments and opinions around them did and do, and from these I created my boundaries and the definitions of my life.

The good thing about this is that I created this and all my life, so I can be the change, if I am willing. And so can you, if you are open to that, again proving that you and I have, and that we have had, this power all along. I was just unaware, asleep if you will, and I used it differently, to create a story of *not being loved, lack* and *less than.*

When you are awake in the dream of perception there are still people, places, things, thoughts, circumstances, things to accept, things to surrender to, things to allow, and actions to take – and then there are your feelings about them – and these are two separate things. Only I had been perceiving all this as if they were connected.

If you're struggling here, read on, there will be actual, real, concrete examples for you to ponder. Right about now your ego is saying something, I am sure. And right about here is where the forks in the road begin.

The Crossroads

I REALIZE THAT WHERE I am at now is a culmination of lifetimes of perceptions and the feelings that arose from them, and that I am just going to feel what I am going to feel. However, now I can *choose* how I am going to *respond*. So from this point forward I will create a new Response-Ability. That new *Response-Ability* is my *responsibility* to observe and be aware of my feelings, and to be fully present with them as much and as often as I can with as little opinion or judgment as possible. I will get into the needs behind the feelings later.

So this is where it gets goofy. How, in today's world of instant everything and distractions galore, do you accomplish this?

I have found that for myself, these three key components work best: a balance of letting go of judgment of self (in other words, having compassion for myself), living with purpose, and having fun.

If you struggle with this, please feel free to connect with me. This is not a one-size-fits-all suggestion; these are three things that as I brought them to the forefront of my life have helped me to balance my life. A hint here: in order for me to do this I had to stop condemning myself, or at the very least, stop thinking I need to do something to receive, and remind myself that I Am enough. But more on *receive* later.

It always starts and ends with me. No one and no thing – nothing – can or does control you/me. That is an illusion, your/my illusion. By the way, it *was* my illusion. In reality, all beings are energy, are free, always have and always have had freedom of choice. This cannot be taken from you, as it is yours by birthright and was given to you when you first came into being as a pure energy. It is known as the Universal Law of Free Will. You can choose as you desire, when and what you desire. This is a key concept to grasp.

I don't know about you, but I am choosing to exercise it in my favor now, instead of by default, as I did in the past. Although it is inherently yours, you can surrender it, as I did, without consciously being aware of my story at the time. I don't know about you, but I was never taught this, and I/we just forgot, as we hid our freedom in plain sight in our story of our life. Hey, at least we were smart enough to keep it close by while we played follow the leader! I think we did that on purpose, as we are pretty smart beings, as you will soon see if by some chance you have not already perceived this for yourself.

So here is my process. I hope you benefit from it as much as I did, and still do.

One of the easiest and quickest ways for me to tell where I am with my perception, before I respond to anything or anyone, is by paying attention to the feelings within me, my awareness of how I feel. For me, my feelings are my best indicator. I am in no way telling you what to do here. I want you to find what works best for you, as you may have something different that works better for you. Listen to your own heart and Soul.

I begin by asking myself, am I expanding or am I contracting? If I feel I am expanding, I ask myself why and have a brief look. If not, and I am contracting, I ask myself why. Once I understand why I am contracting, usually due to a need of mine not being met, then I will specifically ask myself, *what* need is not being met?

Next I will ask myself, is there a desperate or despairing energy around the need? (Hint: If you feel yourself contracting, there is a desperate, clingy or despairing energy there.) Your assignment, should you choose to accept it, is to be as honest with yourself as you can, while being gentle with yourself. Condemning thoughts of self will just keep you contracted.

Next, as I see and feel into the despairing energy, I compassionately ask myself if I can release the desperation or despair around the real need. You are not letting go of your legitimate need, just the despairing energy around it. The opinion or judgment you are making about it is what usually causes you to attach to it in that desperate way. By asking these questions, you wake up in the dream of perception.

From there, I can choose a new response with decisive and deliberate awareness. I develop the awareness by taking a brief moment to breathe, see how I feel and where I am feeling it, and then ask myself some key questions. This helps me to observe myself from a neutral and compassionate place.

Sometimes it helps me to just recognize where I'm at. Doing that in and of itself releases stuck energy so I can allow my life. Remember, energy wants to just move through you. By the way, that is another Universal Law: Energy is always in motion, and wants to be in motion.

Before we get to the questions, let me define three words and show you how they saved me a lot of grief by my definitions. They helped me receive life, my life, as it was and always is flowing through me.

9

Terms of Endearment
in Receiving Life

aka Releasing Resistance

LET'S FIRST TALK about this term *resistance* that has received such a bad rap. Without resistance we would have little indication that things are subtly off. Resistance is useful for us in many ways, alerting us to danger, to something or someone or some circumstance that is not good for us, etc. Resistance is also a bodily indicator that can tell you that you are about to embark into, or are already in, something that is at a higher level of consciousness/understanding than you're at now.

The big Question for me here is, do I perceive it that way, or am I seeing it as that somebody or something is doing it to me? When everything hits the fan, we know all too well that life is amiss. But usually, if you're paying attention, way before the big blow-up there is resistance along the trail. And I don't know about you, but that was a news flash to me. So you mean all that stuff I had just put my head down and plowed through, and past, were little hints that the freight train was a-comin'? Where was the class on this in school? My head would still be round on top had I known that.

My new view goes something like this – and keep in mind, this is my view. Please speak with and be with your own Soul and see how and what you are guided to, for you. This is not a game of follow the leader. You are your own amazing individual. BE IT.

I view resistance as this little boy I am walking through life with. When he is scared, he is gently tugging at the back of my shirt. If I slow down, I can hear the whisper of a shy, scared young boy before it becomes a scream. He is usually, though not always, saying I'm scared of XYZ. Then I stop, breathe, and listen to see what is coming up in and for him/me.

Of course the boy is me, but since I chose that split a long time ago, him being outside of me (or so he seems), I use it to my advantage now. We calm ourselves until he is one with me again. How do I do that, you ask? Just have a compassionate conversation around what's coming up, all day every day. It's that easy and quick. We do it when we drive, shower, exercise, cook, write, well you get the point, a lot.

OK, enough on that. I just figured it was worth saying. On to definition time. Again, remember, these are my perceptions/definitions now.

ACCEPT – To accept, for me, means Be Open to All Possibilities, the Whole You, and everything it brings.

Energetically speaking, you can't deny anything on a level or frequency without denying all that's on that level or frequency. Fortunately, the converse is also true. When you accept that All is Possible, it becomes so for you. If you're confused, refer back to Chapter 5.

Let me explain. A legitimate need is money. And you happen to need more of it. Let's say a job comes along that your Soul is saying yes to, and you just can't for the life of you explain why it would be saying yes to this when your ego is saying, "It pays $11 an hour? You're kidding, right? We usually make $100 an hour." Well if you deny it or overlook it without any consideration of what your Soul/higher self is telling you, you have just said to your Soul, "Hey, thanks, but no thanks, I don't need an abundance of that." Abundance is then blocked on that level. It may well be about the lesson and not the money.

Now you may have applied to many jobs/positions and only received one or received many responses. This is where you need to take the time to get clear and pick the one that *feels* right. I will give some real life examples that happened to me later towards the end of the book, and what it cost me by not getting clear so I could communicate with my Soul. The point here is: Never say no. Accept all gifts and then pick the one that **feels** right for you. And here's the rub – sometimes there may be but one choice and it seems so wrong to your ego, but you know in your heart it's the right choice. Follow your heart. It knows. Surprises come in all forms, shapes and sizes.

This journey is about our Soul's growth, not your bank account. That is a reflection of how aligned you are with your Soul. This same principle can be applied to wanting a friend(s) or a partner to share life with in a relationship, business or otherwise. Put your Soul first, and everything else will follow.

Hence the Grand Design of Life. My good friend Nancy told me, "You can't take any physical thing with you to the other side, but what you can take is what you have learned in this lifetime, or what draws you closer to your Soul."

This is my only priority in life and I commit to it every day, day in and day out. The most important thing to me is, how do I show up? Am I showing up with the whole me – the good, the bad and the ugly, and not judging it – or am I compart-mentalizing, trying to show only what I think is my good side?

I can't tell you the immense joy and fun this course of action has brought me. You must, of course, realize that my definition of success is Joy and Fun.

SURRENDER – To surrender, for me, means Innocence.

We are all innocent to life and what it will bring. Tomorrow will come, and it will bring what it's going to bring. By no means does this mean that you are a victim. We play some part in every aspect of our lives, but it's bringing what it's bringing and we will have to make a choice – accept it, or choose to resist. Even if you transition to the next world tomorrow, life (a new life) still came for you, but from there on you will be beyond time. (Yet even in death there is usually resistance, due to regrets, fears, attachment, unfinished business, beliefs about it, etc.)

Resistance is futile, but yet I/we do it. A hint here: It is much easier for things to pass through you when you don't resist, including death. This also includes financial hardships, all dis-ease and well, let's just say pretty much everything. For example, in the process of re-learning and re-membering my Soul lesson of true humility and kindness (the example above, in the section on acceptance regarding money, which will be elaborated on later in the book) I resisted for about two months, and boy, was that painful.

Then I was brought to this place where there was no other choice for me but to surrender and turn myself over to my Soul, as nothing I tried was working. Of course I dropped the ball on different things after that, but my Soul went easy on me in my slow uptake in my remembering lessons that followed, as it knew I was honest and sincere about my surrender. It only hits you hard when you don't listen – that's usually the cumulative effect of years of resistance. We will also elaborate on honesty with yourself and your Soul later in the story. As grace would have it, many doors started opening after that, and you can bet your booty I am now humble and kind to one and all, especially to myself.

ALLOW – To allow, to me, means Grace – the grace to let things flow and allow life to be as it is going to happen anyway. We can't control it, but we *can* control our *response* to it.

Not until very recently did I realize and embody this. I had been accustomed to believing that my power of everything, including Response-Ability, lay outside of myself and depended on what others did or said.

Grace, being another Divine Law of the universe, can only be used in complete sincerity and honesty with self. But here is the kicker: It is and was there all along, I just did not know how to operate myself within that law of the universe. And who's kidding who? Basically I had very little knowledge of the laws, and humbly I say, the more I learn, the more I realize the less I know. And that's OK, I have accepted that, and am allowing my journey to gracefully unfold. This was so, not because I did not want to, but because I had not clearly and completely understood or made contact with my Soul. Once I did, it was game on.

Once you do understand and realize your connection with your Soul, you will never want to lie to yourself or your Soul. You just can't. I'm not really sure how to explain this feeling, but you just won't want to, it will not feel right. If you tell yourself (which is really your Soul) that you're going to do something and you don't follow through, you move into an energetic space of dis-grace, much like dis-ease. It feels like you're just left of center and things just aren't quite flowing. The law of Grace, for me, became this knowing that my Soul is me and I it. And it cannot, nor would it ever, let me down. We are and always were inseparable. I just relaxed into that. I discovered this when I made the decision to be completely honest with myself about all things, not just the things I was comfortable with.

Here are some key questions I have learned to ask myself to enable me to observe myself with less judgment and receive life. But first, my take on blame. Please remember, this is my view of the word blame and how I used it. I, however, thought it might be beneficial to explain this, as it is what helped me unravel my story.

What is blame? The definition according to Siri is: To assign responsibility for fault and/or attribute or assign wrong. So first off, to assign anything is to put it outside of yourself. And if you are putting it on yourself, that is OK if it's done with compassion and self-love, not self-recrimination.

My definition of blame is: A perceived organizing (my story) of miscellaneous circumstances, people and/or events and stringing them together with my perceptions and beliefs (my story) with some sort of conclusion that supports, again, my story.

Bam!!! I call this my string theory of life, or in layman's terms, my line of B.S. that I would tell myself to keep the constructs of the story line of my play, and the life I was living at the time, intact.

The moment you assign an opinion or judgment and responsibility (your Response-Ability) away to anything or anyone outside of yourself is the moment in which you are giving your power of creation away. You are free to do this, I just don't know why one would want to, unless of course I/they were unaware. But if you have gotten this far in this blessed book, then, my friend, you are aware.

This is where the whole premise of forgiveness comes in. It's not for the other; it's so I can find myself and my power and where I left it last.

For example, if I am angry at another or at some situation, and I choose to forgive, it is a release, allowing the energy to flow for me, so I can take back my power from where I left it with someone or something.

It just so happens that it releases both parties, only sometimes one person doesn't choose to recognize this. This is where you have to really be in your awareness and watch out for those pesky expectations and energetic hooks.

I don't know about you, but I have habitually left my power scattered about with people, places, events, circumstances, etc. I have had to learn to re-collect it in my compassionately paying attention to what I am observing and feeling in the moment.

The next question I had to ask myself was: What was the safety requirement I was trying to fulfill using blame? Blame can't keep you safe, this I know now, but boy, I sure used it for just that. So I had to ask myself: How, where, why and in what way did I believe that it kept me safe? For me, it allowed me to rest comfortably on and in my story of putting my power outside of myself.

As I examined this closely, I realized that I'd had this belief for as long as I could remember. I also realized that everything and everyone in my life backed it up – my family, friends, preachers, teachers, and so on. Thus I had created an existence of people, places, things and experiences outside of myself, out of my control, and outside of my ability – my Response-Ability – that were responsible for my life being as it was. Or so I thought.

Sometimes we leave our power hidden in plain sight. The next paragraph will explain one of my favorite old hiding places in plain sight. And here is a hint to expedite your process in realizing that you have, and have had, your power all along, and that you in fact already do and always did embody it. In taking 100% responsibility for your life, do your best to not blame or judge or condemn yourself. This will not lead you to allowing your life. Only acceptance, aka releasing the resistance, will. For me, moving through the process of unconditionally loving, accepting and trusting myself exactly as I am was and is the cornerstone to true joy.

So back to my favorite hiding place. I find that for me, sometimes (OK, who are we kidding, more than sometimes) I have left my power there within that split me, or ego so to speak, by condemning or judging myself. When I go back to that moment, it's almost funny now. My ego is standing there with its hand out as if to say, "Are you looking for this?" My power, that is. And it's, like, lovingly laughing with me and I am, like, this isn't funny anymore, and he says to me, so stop giving it to me, and I jokingly say, see ya later. It's just a process. I am learning not to judge, but to allow it.

Then came the big question that I then asked myself: I wonder ... What would my life be like if I never blamed anyone, or anything, not even myself, for what's happening in my life?

Let's face it, life is going to happen anyway. What if I give it permission to happen to me? To allow moms, dads, grandparents, siblings, children, jobs, co-workers, money, clients, love, hate, etc., to come and go as they wish? Because from what I can see over the past fifty-three years, clearly they do anyway, with or without my inter-fearance. And no, I did not spell that wrong. Clearly, the word *fear* is in that word with good reason.

So I had to ask myself: What am I afraid of here? What is the safety requirement, aka need, that I am insisting be in place before I can be, do, have or allow something? If I would just allow life, I would give life, my life, permission to carry on expediently and efficiently with certainly less obstruction, aka resistance, from me. So I asked myself this question: What if I accept my journey as just that, a journey? Not something I have to judge or make a certain way. What if my healing could be summed up in one word: Acceptance? Just accepting how I feel, with absolutely no one and no thing to blame or judge, not even myself? The bigger question was, could I accept, surrender and allow that?

Not so easy, you say. But likes, dislikes, opinions and judgments are of no concern to me when my Soul's and my happiness is on the line. Think about those questions. If only you knew who you really are, and the love and light you really carry on this journey! You are your Soul, and your Soul is you. You are in God, and God is in you.

Oh, sure, most of us are well aware of our imperfections because they were always pointed out for us, and the good points, well, not so much. But the fact remains that in speaking with hundreds of thousands of individuals just like you and me, we all had ten times the good things in our value and in our lives. Remember, I *did* get that regents diploma and a good score on my SAT's, as well as many other victories and accomplishments. It was just a matter of my perception, what I chose to focus on. And I don't know about you, but I was not taught to see my own good, only my shortcomings, and was told, you could do better.

OK, so that was then and this is now. Now I focus on the good and do not see anything as bad. Hard to believe, you say? Not my issue. I am just saying how it is for me now, from my perspective, with my new Response-Ability. This does not mean I am an emotionless drone. Nothing could be further from the truth. I just do my best to not judge it or have an opinion about it. I know what you're saying, it must be boring. I assure you, if you were in my life, that is not a word you would use to describe me.

Herein lies the key to my life, that I missed: The Good.

We will go into this in a bit, but for the moment, focus on the good within you. Don't believe me. Do it. Make a list, an honest list of the things in your life over all your years and you will see that, like it or not, after looking back – with hindsight being what it is, 20-20 – you will see that you are far more good than otherwise. You just never stopped to look at yourself with an eye of acceptance of who and what you are. And don't be hard on yourself. Few do this, as few are taught this.

10

My Dad's Infinite Wisdom

OK, ON TO THE KEY that I missed. Not only was my perception skewed, but as I said, my focus was usually on my shortcomings, not on my accomplishments or successes. My dad, in all his infinite wisdom and intuition, knew that I was so much more than I was expressing, and now I realize how much this must have frustrated him – hence the angst between us. I was constantly shown what was wrong and told that I could do better. So in my own perception I thought that I was not good enough, stupid, I just couldn't get anything right, and the list goes on. I also made an *assumption*, and you know how those go. It was that I was *not loved*.

Now, looking back, I see the wisdom in his words and I understand his frustration and can appreciate his tenacity for not allowing me to say *I don't know*. For every time that thought is put into spoken word, you give your power away to whatever situation you're in at that moment, and you're claiming your lack of something. Without getting into more laws of the universe, I will just say this.

The mighty AUM (OM) vibration creates our world. The vibration of it and the spoken word has three manifestations: Creation, Preservation, and Destruction. I have learned to speak wisely and in my favor.

So let's break this down with a role play and roll the flashback. I will set the stage. He is helping me with my homework and it goes something like this:

Dad: No! That's not right! Come on, you know better!

Me: I *don't* know.

Dad: I don't know is not an answer! You know better!

And on it would go, sometimes for hours, getting tougher and tougher, it seemed, with my emotions running high and my skewed perceptions in place. I never understood why it would go on for so long. I now realize that what it really was, was a man with great intelligence, a great gut intuition, and infinite patience. He knew that I was so much more, and he would not quit on me, even when I had quit on myself. How could he? He was God the father in action in my life, he loved me beyond words. I just never saw it then, as it was expressed in a way I did not understand, as I had no knowledge of his wounds, upbringing, issues, etc.

As I stated earlier, I, myself, gave up on me. My dad and mom never did. It was just the perception I chose, due to a feeling, which was then followed by the assumption that I was not loved. And thus ensued the life that I created from this assumption. There is no judgment here. I simply at the time did not know better.

My dad was a man who did the very best he could with what knowledge and experience he had, his hurts, and with the love that he was or was not given. The fact remains that I don't know what he experienced in his life. We never talked about that stuff. My parents were not taught to express and share feelings, so how was I supposed to know? I, we, you and me, we couldn't, I assumed, because I was not given explanation behind the behavior.

The really great thing about getting clear in this process for yourself is that when you shift, so do they. You will get the acknowledgement, love, understanding, attention, etc. You will never see it coming. It will just show up one day when you least expect it. There was this one phone call when I called my parents and only my dad was home, and so we chatted a bit. And there it was, big as life – he said he was so proud of me and the things I have done and that he is sure I will do. He said – and I am paraphrasing because I can't remember verbatim what he said – "I would have never done the things you did or in the way you did, it's just too far outside of my comfort zone of what I know."

I can tell you this: I will for sure explain how I am feeling and why to my children. If I am scared, frustrated, angry, they will know I am, and why, because I will share my vulnerability with them. I would never deny them that experience, as that would not serve them well. Protection and/or being the male protector is a dominant trait in males, and ego loves to use it to keep life in separation, separating others and things from you, as well as you from them. I realize now that by sharing all of myself, I am in my power and I also empower another.

I innately knew this and perceived this then, as a child. And so I interpreted what I was experiencing as *not love,* or at the very least, not the love I wanted in the way I wanted it. The truth was that at that point in my young life I had forgotten the original play that we, Creator and I, wrote back before I entered this place. In the manual wisdom notes, which like I said earlier I left behind, but found recently, I had stated that this was how my dad was going to remind me of who I was, the light that I carry, and help me to reclaim my power. Lo and behold, it worked.

11

Second Chances

SINCE I DIDN'T GET IT the first time around, but was earnestly seeking, my Soul and life blessed me with the same opportunity again. Say what? Surely you think I'm kidding, right? I can assure you, I am not. So to top this all off, the whole shebang came full circle again, as life so loves to do for you, to see if you will find a new Response-Ability. If you are a true seeker your Soul will *present opportunities* for you to take full responsibility for your life and claim your power back. Simply put, to wake up, and allow yourself to fully embody it within you, the physical vessel.

On an important side note: As I am writing this, I am understanding many things about my journey that if I would have understood earlier, could have saved me much grief. So I figure I will share. The words *present* and *opportunities* are in bold and italicized above for a reason. I am giving you fair warning: As your Soul brings you opportunities, they may come with disguises that look to your human side *far* from a *present* or an *opportunity*. But I assure you, they are. And this, my friend, is where the rubber meets the road, to see if you will make a different choice.

It did so in my second marriage, with my wife being the mirror instead of my dad, as I made sure I avoided contact with him, except on surface topics. And don't you know, she was every bit as capable as he, and even more so. As we all know, it is difficult to hide when you're in a close mirror relationship like a marriage. I know how much I sometimes frustrated her, as she communicated that, only she did it in a way that I did not recognize, know, understand or approve of – how convenient! – so I could judge and blame once again, and continue to put my power outside of myself if I chose. On occasion I could I see it as a present or opportunity, but I for sure struggled, as I am sure many of us do.

And so it went. I made the choice to connect my perceived wounds that I believed came from her and my dad to my already formed perceptions, thus backing up my assumption of my core story that I was not loved. I now realize that nothing could have been further from the truth on both of their accounts, but I just couldn't see past all of my perceived hurt, since that was how I really felt, and that was what I truly believed, as that was my level of Response-Ability then. Since it was how I felt and believed, I assumed that it was real, as that was what I was basing my whole life upon, those beliefs, needs, feelings and perceptions.

Of course, in doing that, so ran the course of that relationship. It ran from moments of joy and happiness to, well, let's just say, not so much. However, fortunately for me, we remained in communication and she remained steadfast and strong, which kept me true to course. She and I continued to play our parts: she as the mirror, and I manned up to change myself. A funny thing happened, though. As I did, she did as well – or was it the other way around? Well, who knows – in my eyes we are equal Souls with equal love and equal ability to claim our power, and so we did.

I now realize that those earlier thoughts were skewed by my perceptions and by the faulty belief system that I had created. So now I have more quest-ions (questions) for myself. I know what you're thinking – more bleeping questions, doesn't this guy ever stop? No. Hopefully you're seeing the pattern here. Questions are a way to reverse engineer your way out of the dream. Also the word *quest* is in question, as well as *ion*, which is, in a sense, an atom, which is the very fabric of everything. You can't make this stuff up. There are bread crumb trails everywhere, if you slow down and look.

If my own perceptions were not real, then what was? If they were not real, only perceptions – then holy crap, Marie, my whole life is and was made up. And not only made up, but made up of perceptions of *less than* that were based on inaccurate assumptions.

The good thing here is that if I created it, which I did, then I can also uncreate it, and re-create a new and different life. When I realized this it was like the lights went on and I could see the truth.

Whenever you feel life is happening **to** you rather than **through** you, you know your perception is off. Anger can only come from vexed expectations, aka opinions, judgments, and/or beliefs about how something or someone should or shouldn't be. Right there, stop and breathe, feel all of what you're feeling, all the way through you. Just be in your awareness and see if you can avoid the standard "this is happening to me" knee-jerk response. Use a different Response-Ability and see if you can see it from a different perspective or perception. Look to see how, where, why and about what you are putting your power outside of yourself, and onto who or what. See which of your need(s) is/are not being met, and look for the desperate, clingy or despairing energy that is attached to what you are feeling. See if you can get out of judgment, and recognize your own part in it. Take 100% responsibility for your own thoughts, words and actions, and get out of the idea that somebody or something is doing it to you. In essence, this is energetically separating you from the circumstance, person, place or thing. Then see if you can allow life to just be, letting go of insisting that it be a certain way in a certain time. Just surrender and let it flow through you. This is all your Soul is asking of you, and if I can do this, believe me, you can do this.

12

Life Is Happening Anyway

L IFE IS EITHER GOING to happen *to* you or *through* you, but rest assured, it will happen. And it is your perception that dictates in which of those ways you will receive it. The realization I hope we will all have here is that life is made up and that we are the ones that make it up, we are the creators of our own life and destiny.

I am aware that I/we do have the ability to create our life, and that we are creating it moment by moment, thought by thought, though I often still do struggle with this and create through default perceptions, not a relaxed present awareness. I realize that embodiment of this belief is for me a life process, and I will do my best to gracefully move through it. I know that some will buck this thought or idea because of some hurt, pain or tragedy, and that's OK—you are where you are, and it truly is all good. All I ask is that you look at where your focus is, and what your choice is about that, regarding what you are telling yourself. Is it within you or outside of you, on some other person, place, circumstance or thing?

To that I will also say that our memory of the past fades for a reason, and this is a natural, organic process. Oh, and how we choose to fight this! People *choose* to remember hurts, wounds, pain, etc. People think that by not forgetting, this will keep them safe, and that whatever it was won't happen again.

Good luck with that! I would love to know how that's working for you, and even if by some chance it has kept it or them away, what is or did it cost you – not only psychologically, but even physically? I've never heard it said, "Hey so and so, that cancer (or any dis-ease) looks good on you." Get my point? If not, think about it. Resentments and regrets, their price tag is quite high.

Resistance is the illusion of safety and/or control. You don't go through suffering. It passes through you, as does all of life, if you let it. It is only when I stand in resistance to life that I feel pain.

This is why some people hate exercise. It is you against some form of resistance exercise movement, and most individuals dislike the discomfort or pain that is usually associated with it. Here is a hint: If you resisted it less you would enjoy it more, with twice the benefit. Anyway, don't get me started on this!

I have tried to the best of my ability to take life moment by moment, and in so doing it helps me to perceive differently and bring this next thought into a realized embodiment within my humanness. All I mean by that, in layman's terms, is that I am Awake within the dream of life here on this planet. I no longer suffer the amnesia experience of humanity.

I remember fully who I Am and my joy and light I share. If there is any dis-ease in any way in my life, I created it, and I will un-create it, because I am fully aware that *I have the ability to do both.* And I don't know about you, but I prefer ease. Also, on a side note, you can ask your Soul for help with clearing past energy and/or dis-ease issues of any kind. If you do, it would be wise to be humble and sincere.

Regarding my awareness, I realize now that all is Creator, all of life is God, and that you can't compartmentalize Creator/God. God/Creator is *everywhere*, in *everything* and *everyone*. No one and no thing – *nothing* – is to blame for how I feel. If that were so, it would be outside of me, and I would have no choice, no power to control how I feel. But I now am awake, so I know better. I know that I do have this power.

Remember, I have the ability to create both ways, so I would be feeling just the way I feel, no matter how different my life might be. It is a choice, your and my choice, to feel what I/we choose to feel. Feelings change when they do, circumstances change when they do, and no amount of persons, places, things or circumstances changes how I feel or *is the reason why I feel.* (There are plenty of wealthy people who **Choose** to be miserable.) As I said, and this is worth repeating – if this were so, I would be placing my power outside of myself. I am awake, and I no longer can or will do this. What you do, is your choice. I know it seems like a lot of change, but you can do this, I assure you. If I did this, you can, too.

Just so we are clear, you can't do this halfway and say, well, if this or that happens I will feel good or bad. Or if so-and-so does this, it or they will make me feel a certain way. Bad or good, you are putting your power outside yourself if it's not all you.

Nobody and no thing can make you feel a certain way. Only you can. That's your power. Since you have it, why not use it wisely? I know what you're saying, I can hear it now – how the heck am I *not* supposed to get angry, scared, upset, frustrated, sad, happy, etc.?

I did not say you won't feel these things. What I'm saying is that you are disconnecting from your

Soul or highest self when you direct a judgment or opinion towards others, circumstances, or yourself. I have all these feelings, needs and emotions. I just realize it fast and say, oh, there's that feeling again. OK. I am outside of myself again, usually with my perception due to an opinion and/or judgment. **I take a breath, notice what I'm feeling, and draw my awareness back into harmony by whatever means necessary, using my Response-Ability, through focused choice.** Then I might ask myself, self/ego, what need is not being met?

If you are confused, re-read Chapter 8. But before you do, make a sincere request to your Soul for the wisdom to understand and comprehend this in a way that allows you to apply it in your life. Knowledge is not wisdom until it can be applied usefully and practically in your world. This is why I wrote this book, in hopes it would simplify what has been made complicated, and so you can apply it in your day-to-day life and find real lasting joy and happiness.

You must ask sincerely. My teachers used to ask me, do you want to be right, or light? If you choose right, let me know how that works for you and how happy you are all the time. For me, true creation is my joy and radiance of all of me in the world, without definition or limits. And by all of me I mean the good, the bad and the ugly. This is not judgment, but a statement to describe in our limited vernacular the infinite *we are* and *Creator is*. As we are all things, Creator is all things, as we are part of Creator and Creator is in us and everything else.

This must be so, because we are all sons, daughters (some of us both), creations of Creator, a subject for a different day. Creator/God would never say to one of his sons or daughters, *you* are great, and to the other, *you* are bad. Creator did not fill me with more love than someone else. Last time I checked, our hearts were filled with the same amounts of love and Creator said, now go and let me see what you can do with this gift (aka your life) I have given you. Creator is neutral and loves all alike. All of our vessels are filled with the same amount of love, without exception. It is our learned labels, opinions, and judgments that have formed our limited perceptions, such as that some are evil and some are not. I would love to see how someone could justify killing another to a totally benevolent society.

This brings to mind a story. Yes, a story – hey, at least it's not another question.

I remember hearing one time there was this whole civilization that had to leave its planet. So off they went, bringing their people to and fro. One day they came upon Earth. Since it matched the requirements necessary to sustain them, they decided to drop in and converse with its inhabitants to see if it might be a place they could stay. In so doing, they noticed a fair amount of doing away with one another.

So the leader asked many individuals of earth to explain this to her and her male counterpart. It was not a concept they would or could understand. They understood the laws of energy and matter clearly. They knew all too well that if you do something to someone else, it will affect you the same way, equally. Another word for it is karma, a human word made up to describe energy and its boomerang effect. That said, the visitors decided to move on with their civilization. However, the last person the visitors spoke to, a young man named Jordan, asked a question of the visitors. With a small tear running down his face, he asked, "Why can't you stay?" He had bonded quickly with them, and was sad that they were leaving.

They replied, "Even though we can sense and see everywhere at all times all around the globe, and just as easily directly behind us, we would rather not have to use this ability to see if someone is going to harm us. We prefer to live peaceably with one another and accept our differences, surrender to our Souls, and allow ourselves and others to just be." They knew that they were, as we all are, the very fabric of everything.

Seeing that Jordan was upset, the leader reached out to him and gave him a hug. She then whispered something in his ear that brought a great smile to his face. He was not allowed to tell what it was, for if he did, its magic would be diminished for him. Rumor has it, though, that she told him they would keep a special eye on us and our planet until we finally figure it out. I suspect there is much truth to this story, but you can decide that for yourself.

OK, story time is over. Back to the nitty gritty.

It is the judgment that acts like glue and holds your story together. It starts with us judging ourselves, based on outside opinions. **Hint here – so ending it must also start with us.**

You ask, what about how I feel? We feel because we were created as feeling beings, and our feeling body is closely connected to our emotional body, hence the confusion and the easy triggers. Take a moment or two or three and examine this next thought regarding feelings. This is how I see it now – however, this is not how I perceived it as a child, or even not that long ago.

Regarding my feelings – perhaps, just perhaps, the connections I have made between my perceptions and my feelings, by my own choice, based no doubt on a need – perhaps I just *imagined* there is a connection, through my learned perceptions and belief systems. And perhaps, just maybe, even in reading and/or saying these words, I am becoming aware of my perception *now*, as I read this.

The action I took, and am still taking, to change my life and awaken within the dream is that I use my power of choice to imagine a different connection, through a different perception and focus. What is the focus, you ask? It is that nothing and no one is creating my life. I Am the one creating. I Am creator, preserver and destroyer. So I may as well create in my favor, preserve as I wish, and let go of whatever and whoever is not serving me. It just makes sense. The truth here is, it all serves. The question is, can I refrain from judging it, so that when it's done serving, I and it can be allowed to go peaceably?

Most people are not aware that they can change their beliefs and perceptions. They don't understand that they can observe something differently. If they did, they would have to admit that they are in their power and then do something other than chase their tail with the same story over and over, day in and day out. You can argue this if you like, but you'd better have a good story for the one of why we still kill one another on this planet.

Take a moment and absorb this next statement. As you become aware of your perception in this moment, you are no longer lost or trapped within it. One who is dreaming does not know it's a dream. The moment you perceive the dream is the very moment you are no longer dreaming, but awake within the dream.

Why is this so important? Because there is a huge difference between experiencing something (your story, your life) and being lost or trapped in it, feeling like you can't control it.

To be clear here, it is not control of life in general that I mean, but of *your* life, *you*, through your awareness of how you feel in the moments of it, and your thoughts about it, and your response to it. This is your Response-Ability, your power, your divine birthright, the freedom of choice. Freedom of choice is the secret to the game that most are not aware of. And it is not just a choice, it is a Divine Law of our universe, God's Grace in action.

13

Where the Rubber
Meets the Road

I SAID I WOULD give real life examples. I have chosen to share all of myself with you, even though it is scaring the bejesus out of me.

When I was finishing up this book the biggest wildfire in California history burned from Santa Paula and Ventura in the southeast to Santa Barbara in the northwest, where I reside. What followed after that was everyone's worst nightmare —too much rain, too fast, and the mud began to flow, wiping out parts of beautiful Montecito.

This was a place I had purposely moved to in order to start over, only a couple of months before. To say the least it was, and as I write this it still is, quite an experience for all affected, and certainly more so for some. I am pointing this out as this experience challenged me and still is, as I am sure it did all of us. Had I not applied what I have spoken of here in this text, it surely would have been even more difficult for me.

The fire did not burn me directly or where I live, but let's just say I hope that's as close as I ever come to that. However, it did present a formidable challenge to me, and manage to scorch my ego. It managed to bring up every fear and wound that was willing to rear its head, and of course there were plenty. Funny thing, though, I never lost hope till, yup, you guessed it – till the rain.

That Tuesday at 2:45 a.m. I awoke in the dead of night, shot bolt upright and was like, what the heck is going on, and things got real. I could feel the fear in the air, thick like a fog marine layer rolling in off the Pacific. I stood there looking across the valley at Montecito, watching the torrents of rain and wind. All I could do was send love and prayers to that side of town as I stood there helpless, as I knew that right in that moment my fellow brothers and sisters were being washed down the hillside with all their belongings, cars, homes, pets, children, you get the idea. I did not know what to do, as who does in these situations? One just does their best. Should I disconnect from it, as if I could? Do I go see if I can help? Or wait it out? Daylight came quickly and it was clear that the mudslide had washed out a good part of Montecito and everything in its path, right over the 101 freeway, and even out to sea.

What I was feeling on the inside was surreal. As I said, I was not actually in the physically affected area, so this next representation is not referring to me being in the path of the mud.

For myself, the mud did not wash away all of what I described earlier for others – though I was in deep pain from that, as I could feel their loss, sorrow, anguish, desperation and fear – but it felt just as physically destructive to me. It felt as if all my dreams were washed away, crushed if you will. There are and were many blessed people that lived in Montecito that employed a great many of us and there it was, the Holy Shazam moment, my income stream wiped out. I was angry at myself at first for feeling that, as I well knew that there were others far worse off than I was, but then I applied a different perception of appreciation and gratitude and moved past that as quickly as I could.

I was motivated to be the best me I could be, to be of assistance to my fellow brothers and sisters, rather than give away my power to a circumstance as I had so often done in my past. It was the same for me in New York when the Trade Center came down, and when Hurricane Sandy hit, but somehow this experience in Santa Barbara just broke me. I think being alone, out of money and on my own compounded it for me. However, by choice as I was guided to this path by my Soul, it was scary, yes, but impossible? NO.

I have learned that for the heart to break is a natural process that sometimes happens in life. To try to protect it from hurt and/or keep it from breaking is not productive, and to harbor such a heartache will surely break you later on. Allowing is no easy feat if perception is skewed. People often say, "Oh, I'm out of alignment, I can't find my alignment." Well it's right where you left it, with whom or whatever, and as Reverend Larry Schellink says, who moved? Surely your Soul and/or Creator did not.

I am reminded of a quote by Suzy Kassem: "Doubt kills more dreams than failure ever will." My whole life I doubted myself and did not believe in myself as much as I would have liked. Every day during the fire and mudslide experience I was wrestling with my doubts and fears, as I am sure many were that day, and in the days to follow, as we all do.

Well after this comeback, I do believe in myself, and I always will. In those moments when it got real that night and in the days to follow, it was my perceptions that were off, and that kicked up my self-doubts to a whole new level of fear I had not known until then.

14

Accept, Surrender, Allow, Receive

aka Release the Resistance

AS I STATED earlier, in Chapter 8, I said I would tell another story that would give real life examples of applying a new Response-Ability. And this is one very close to my heart because it is between myself and my first and best friend here in Santa Barbara, Nancy Keller.

But first a review on resistance. Yes, more repetition, and I'm not apologizing. The term resistance has received a lot of bad rap. Without resistance we would have little indication that things are subtly off or that we are entering something that may or may not serve us. Sure, when everything hits the fan we know all too well that life is amiss. But usually, if you're paying attention, way before the big blow-up there's been resistance along the trail.

Boy, do I wish I would have known that sooner. Like I said earlier, I usually had just put my head down and plowed through and right past all the little hints that the freight train was a-comin'. Yup, my head is flat on top, no hats for me.

I am sharing this story because it has actual realizations from both my friend Nancy and me, about how life just has a way of working out, if you will let, aka allow it. I gleaned a great deal from our conversation one evening during that time of my personal metamorphosis, and it pertains to the earlier statements regarding Accept, Surrender, Allow, and Receive life. In order to receive life, and receive from life, these were the avenues I chose. There is no secret here, I am sure you have heard this before. I simply chose a path that I had seen other really joyful people apply in their lives, and chose to apply it to mine. I recorded the journey in hopes that if there were others seeking, as I was, it might be of some use. For your convenience, here are these definitions again. But first ...

Remember, these are *my* definitions that with *my* perception helped wake *me* up within *my* dream of my life. Feel free to improvise as your wisdom and heart guide you. As you become aware of your perception in this moment, you are no longer lost or trapped within it or the story. Remember, one who is dreaming does not know it's a dream. The moment you perceive the dream, aka wake up within the dream, is the very moment you are no longer dreaming, but are awake within the dream. Why is this so important? Because there is a huge difference between experiencing the expression of something (your story, your life) and being lost or trapped in it, feeling helpless, like you can't control yourself within your life.

Sound like you heard this somewhere before? Good! Then you are paying attention and your Soul must have heard your request to understand this information for yourself, in your own way.

Always remember what you *can* control, *You*. So start with your breath. Begin by just simply becoming aware of your breath and how you are breathing. Start noticing yourself; become aware in the moment of yourself and how you feel. Become aware of how you are showing up in each moment of life.

Now here, again, are those pesky definitions of mine.

ACCEPT – To accept, for me, means Be Open to **All Possibilities, the Whole You**. Energetically speaking, you can't deny anything on a level without denying all that's on that level. Fortunately, the converse is also true. When you accept that All is Possible, it becomes so for you.

Let me explain. A legitimate need is money.

And you happen to need more of it. Well if a job comes along that your Soul is saying yes to, and you just can't for the life of you explain it – your ego is telling you, "It pays $11 an hour? You're kidding, right? We usually make $100 an hour." – well if you deny it or overlook it without any consideration to your higher self, then you have just said to your Soul, "Hey, thanks, but no thanks, I don't need an abundance of that." Abundance is then blocked on that level.

Now you may have applied to many jobs/positions and only received one or received many responses. This is where you need to take the time to **get clear on the meaning of everything we have been talking about thus far,** and pick the one that **feels** right. The point here is: Never say no. Accept all gifts, **allow them,** and then pick the one that **feels** right for you.

And here's the rub – sometimes there may be but one choice and it seems so wrong to your ego, but you know in your heart it's the right choice. Follow that feeling in your heart. It knows. Surprises come in all forms, shapes and sizes.

This journey is about your Soul's growth, not your bank account. That is a reflection of how aligned you are with your Soul. This same principle can be applied to wanting a friend(s) or a partner to share life with in a relationship, business or otherwise. Put your Soul first, and everything else will follow.

Hence the Grand Design of Life. My good friend Nancy told me, **"No one, not even you, can take any material thing with you to the other side. But what you can take is everything your Soul grows by in this lifetime, or that you learn in this lifetime."**

This is my only priority in life and I commit to it every day, day in and day out. I now realize that Life, my life, is offering me everything. It is, however, up to me to reach out past my fears, insecurities, doubts, etc. and take what I desire to grow by in this lifetime. To be clear, this is a process, and something I do daily, all day every day, not something you do for a bit and then you're done. It is a way of life – that is, living awake within the dream.

The most important thing to me is, how do I show up? Am I showing up with the whole me – the good, the bad and the ugly, and not judging it – or am I compartmentalizing, trying to show only what I think is my good side?

I can't tell you the immense joy and fun that staying out of judgment **as much as I can** has brought me. You must, of course, realize that my definition of success is Joy and Fun. I lovingly challenge myself to be Aware in each moment as best I can, all day every day.

SURRENDER – To surrender, for me, means Innocence.

We are all innocent to life and what it will bring. Tomorrow will come, and it will bring what it's going to bring. By no means does this mean you are a victim. We play some part in every aspect of our lives, but it's bringing what it's bringing and we will have to make a **choice** – accept it, or choose to resist. Even if you transition to the next world tomorrow, life (a new life) still came for you, but from there on you will be beyond time. (Yet even in death there is usually resistance, due to regrets, fears, attachment, unfinished business, beliefs about it, etc.)

Resistance is futile but yet I/we do it. **A hint here: It is much easier for things to pass through you when you don't resist, including death. Learn to take the hint that resistance is giving you, and use it to your advantage.** Remember regarding resistance that included in this are financial hardships, all dis-ease and well, let's just say pretty much everything.

For example, in the process of re-learning and remembering my Soul lesson of True Humility and Kindness (the example above, in the section on acceptance regarding money, which will be elaborated on later in the book), I resisted taking that job for about two months. Then I was brought to this place where there was no other choice for me but to Surrender and turn myself over to my Soul, as **no-thing** I tried was working.

Of course I dropped the ball on occasion on different things after that, but my Soul went easy on me in my slow uptake in my remembering lessons that followed, as it knew I was honest and sincere about my surrender. It only hits you hard when you don't listen – that's usually the cumulative effect of years of resistance.

We will also elaborate on honesty with yourself and your Soul later in the story. As grace would have it, many doors started opening after that, and you can bet your booty I am now humble and kind to one and all, especially to **me. Which if you have not figured it out already is where I started, with me.**

ALLOW – To allow, to me, means Grace – the grace to let things flow and allow life to be as it is going to happen anyway. We can't control it, but we *can* control our **response** to it. Is this sounding repetitive? Good, so you're seeing the theme here, I will assume.

Not until very recently did I realize and embody this. I had been accustomed to believing that my power of everything, including response, lay outside of myself and depended on what others did or said.

Grace, being another Divine Law of the universe, can only be used in complete sincerity and honesty with self, **as it is given to you by you, not by something or someone outside of you.**

But here is the kicker: It is and was there all along, I just did not know how to operate myself within that Law of the universe. And who's kidding who? Basically I had very little knowledge of the laws, and humbly I say, the more I learn, the more I realize the less I know. And that's OK, I have accepted that, and am allowing my journey to gracefully unfold.

This was so, not because I did not want to, but because I had not clearly and completely understood or made contact with my Soul. **Note: In case you have missed the theme of the whole Blessed book, it is to start loving on you. Even a little compassion from you to Self goes a long, long way.**

You say, give me an example. OK, you asked for it. If by some chance you've made it this far and you're still reading this literary masterpiece, and you're feeling, let's say, grateful I wrote it, by some chance – make sure the gratitude is directed at **you, NOT me.** Show **your** Soul you appreciate that it brought this information to you how and when it did, and continue this appreciation to your Soul for all of the persons, places and things in your life. Appreciate *you*.

Once I did this, it was game on. Once you understand and realize your connection with your Soul, you will never want to be unkind to or lie to yourself or your Soul. You just can't. I'm not really sure how to explain this feeling, but you just won't want to, it will not feel right. If you tell yourself (which is really your Soul) that you're going to do something and you don't follow through, you move into an energetic space of dis-grace, much like dis-ease. It feels like you're just left of center and like things just aren't quite flowing.

The law of Grace, for me, became this knowing that my Soul is me and I it. **And it cannot, nor would it ever, let me down. EVER**. We are and always were inseparable. Once I understood this, I just relaxed into it. Yes, I may have moved away from my Soul's wisdom at times in my life, based on my own skewed perceptions and belief systems, but it has never let me out of its sight, this I can Assure you.

The same is true for you. I am not special here. We are all created equal. Everything else is an untruth. I know there will be some that will find this difficult to believe, as life has shown them otherwise. But you had best remember who created this, your/my life. I know that I did and Am creating it, and I accept that. Now I can make it what I want, not what others showed me or expected from me in their limited understandings, perceptions and beliefs.

You ask, when did you discover all this? You did, I heard you ask. I discovered this when I made the decision to be completely honest with myself about all things, not just the things I was comfortable with. When I decided to completely Accept life, my life. When I decided to Surrender, totally surrender to life, my life. When I decided to completely Allow life, my life. I will share this story later in the book – don't worry, I will tie it all together.

For now, let's carry these thoughts to the next set of questions. Yes, life is one big question. But first, a story.

15

Change Your Story,
Change Your Life

THE STORY GOES LIKE this. One night Nancy and I went to a free benefit concert that the Santa Barbara Symphony performed for the citizens of Santa Barbara after the fire and mudslide, for the purpose of healing, to lift spirits, and to help form a sense of community. It was string instruments, one percussion, and also a special guest classical guitarist visiting from Spain. The energy for me when we arrived was one of some somberness, as well one might expect.

Classical music has a way of shifting my presence, bringing clarity and peace to my Soul. After the concert, we were both feeling better.

As we drove back we got to talking about life, and our lives. Not just from the time when I arrived in Santa Barbara, but before that as well, when we did not know one another. It went something like this.

We began to share back and forth about lessons learned and about how different people in our lives had given us glimpses into our future lives. Funny thing, we'd both had the same reactions and had thought they were, well, nuts, to say it politely.

For me, it was my dad. He had told me things when I was a young man, sometimes subtly, and sometimes not so much, though not always in an insisting way. He would say, for example, "Ya know, you might want to consider this, just in case of XYZ." Like when he would tell me to save for a rainy day or invest in something other than myself. Of course in my young brilliance I felt like, "Who, me? It can't, it won't ever happen to me." As if I was bulletproof or something. Sometimes I look back and wonder how my parents even dealt with me.

Nancy's story was about the time, years before, that the pastor of her church back in northern California where she had come from had told her that he'd had a vision of her working as a teacher, and had told her that she would work as a teacher one day. "Poor old Pastor," she had thought as she'd listened to him. "He doesn't understand that I am an international author. Why would I want to work in some little classroom, when I am an author who travels all around the world writing books?" She went on to tell how humbled she felt after various things changed in her life and she did become a teacher, and still is, just as her pastor had prophesied.

After she told me the pastor story she told me a story about the financial situation she had been in when she first came to Santa Barbara, and how she'd had to find a job because of an astonishing series of consecutive financially draining events. The one that struck home for me was the K-Mart story, and the chain of synchronistic events to follow.

With her friend Rudy sick, with herself committed to stay in Santa Barbara to help him and thus unable to travel and write books anymore (which had been her longtime passion and career), and with her finances in total collapse and debts mounting, she had begged Creator for help. She had felt fearful and stuck, with no idea what to do. She promised Creator that she would take the first opportunity that came her way, whatever it was, however much or little it paid, regardless of whether she liked it or not, just to get some movement happening, if nothing else.

One day shortly after that, she had pulled up in front of the Goleta K-Mart store, and there in the front window was a red and white sign about four feet tall, blazing out "Help Wanted." Her first reaction was, "No! Not K-Mart!" But she remembered her promise to Creator, she went inside and filled out the application, and was told she would start work the next morning.

She was able to bring herself to a place of being open to all possibilities by Accepting all opportunities that came her way. She Surrendered to life, and trusted Creator. That was the grace moment, where she responded to life with an attitude of Accepting, Allowing, gratitude and trust. And of course she received – not necessarily what she wanted, but what she needed.

After taking the K-Mart job, she applied for and was offered a number of other jobs. She was still working at K-Mart when she was offered a job at Santa Barbara City College, the prestigious community college where she still works today – yes, as a teacher. And on a receiving note, she today – but she couldn't perceive it then – is in a good position in regard to all of life.

OK, so that is example one. Of course we are telling this from hindsight from where she is now. By her Listening, Accepting and Surrendering, she Allowed her life. And what it has brought her has been amazing.

Now here is my story from what happened to me when I first moved to Santa Barbara, before the fire and mudslide.

When I first came to check out this beautiful town, I fell in love with it immediately. I had my game plan in place, or so I thought. I knew who I was going to talk to and why when I came back for good in September, based on the homework I had done on my first visit in July, and the two months of calls I had made that had preceded my first visit. Then I had made more follow-up calls before my return in September. Man, I thought, I've got my bases covered. Riiiiiiiight.

But something was off upon my return. It seemed as though all the doors that I'd thought, or should I say perceived, were open to me, were not.

OK, here we go, Shazam moment number one. Now what? Like any high spirited Soul, I pushed on, went back to the drawing board, and came up with a different approach and plan. I thought to myself, I shall forge on, I'm not letting this stop me. It seemed logical to me, right?

So out I went, with the best of intentions, and there was a little better response, but still not enough to get me to break even. Then one day I was driving to see another potential client and it just so happened that the route took me past Platinum Fitness, which until that moment I hadn't known existed. In my head I heard that still small voice, and it said, go in and talk to him.

(By the way, this had also happened to me in South Lake Union, Seattle when I was there, with another gentleman, Mr. Ivan Salaverry, and his mixed martial arts facility. It worked amazing for both of us, and we are still close friends.)

So after much deliberation with my own Beingness, aka ego, I finally decided to listen to that still small voice within and stop at Platinum Fitness in Summerland. And the long story short, don't you know, lo and behold, Peter and I, well we are cut from a similar cloth, and things were working out well. For those that don't live here in southern California, Summerland abuts Montecito, and most of Platinum's clientele lived in Montecito, as did most of the clients I was serving. Life was grand.

After the fire and the mudslide, back-to-back catastrophes – yes, you know what's coming, you guessed it – Shazam moment number two. Like I said earlier, my income stream was wiped out overnight. I'm thinking, did this just really happen? The odds of two major disasters like this happening right after I moved to this beautiful town were so improbable, as was the fact that all but one of my clients had to evacuate indefinitely. The shock of disbelief slowly crept over me.

OK, back to the Nancy and I car conversation,

which happened after the fire and mudslide classical concert. Nancy, in all her wisdom and wanting to help me, had all these ideas for job opportunities for me to look at, and she was going a mile a minute rattling them off – and I was thinking, "UGH, a job! No way! I work for myself! STOP! I won't do it!" … and on and on I went, in my little head. I was thinking, "But I planned! I pushed! I forged the path, and I worked hard! How can this be?"

It was at that moment that my Soul clearly and sternly spoke to me and said, "Hey, Jackass!" – J.A., as my friend Vincent Cote in New York would say – "You ain't workin' for anyone, not even yourself. So how's that workin' for ya?" And there it was, Bam, big as a house with neon lights. I heard that voice – you know the one I'm talking about – and it said, "If you Dis-Allow anything at any level, you disallow it all." I'm listening and thinking, "What do you mean?" And here it comes, the aha moment. "Let it all come. Accept it all. Take the whole smorgasbord and put it in your lap. Allow it into you, and then pick what feels right."

Right here, I just want to say, is where **staying in the moment is crucial**. Because believe you me, that little voice was saying, "You want us to take the eleven dollar per hour job? You're joking, right?" That voice was not so little by now, and it was screaming, "What about this? What about that? And then there is this other thing!" None of which were in this moment – they were all either in the past or the future. (Your Soul can only be in the now, so if you desire to be in sync with it, be in the moments of Now with it.)

Man, that was not so easy to surrender to, as I went from one pay scale to the other it seemed overnight. And of course I was still feeling sorry for myself and was busy nursing my wounds. But eventually, with Nancy's prodding, I did Accept and Surrender, as I remembered Nancy's brave example and realized that I have a choice, to pick a different Response-Ability. I could try this new road in front of me of Accept, Allow and Surrender, as nothing else was going on anyway.

Just so we are clear here, it took me a couple of months to make this switch. Now I have the rest of my life to master it.

And so I followed the direction I had been given. I filled out many applications and I accepted all opportunities that came to me by Surrendering to life, since it was going to bring what it was going to anyway, and with Creator's grace, I allowed it to flow. And yes, things started to move from there.

As I write these words, am I out of the woods? No, not by a long shot, but it's not over yet. I will continue to choose a better Response-Ability that supports me, my divine plan, and where that divine plan desires to take me. I guess if you want to know how it turns out you will have to continue on to the end.

Like I said, my life is an ever-evolving balance of staying in the moment and creating, as this is what a Soul does. The Soul is going to follow its plan with or without you. Sometimes it even leaves your physical body to do so, as when you transition from great resistance or dis-ease. You just never know what life will bring you tomorrow, or even if it will bring you a tomorrow, so you may as well stay in the present and enjoy it as best you can and make the most of it. All I am saying here is, find a way to agree with the moment. This is not passivity but using the path of least resistance, jumping into the flow of Life, and letting that open the door to possibility.

In the days that followed the mudslide I spent as much time as I could helping out in the community, as I love to do that and it kept me present. As I was helping others, I saw how other people much worse off than I was were handling the situation.

I am renewed. I am lifted up by the resiliency of my fellow brothers and sisters here, and I am in awe of the massive effort and teamwork by everyone who was affected and involved in the clean-up. Yes, the experience did break me. It broke me open to allow the best of me out so I can offer that to the world. My Soul made sure I was going to walk the walk if I was going to talk the talk. To allow the Divine, through me, to bless and multiply all that I Am, all that I have, and all that I share.

16

What My Soul
Knew All Along

OK, TIME FOR a short story regarding my lesson on observation in awareness. Ah, who are we kidding, it's a long story – just keep reading, you'll love it. Who doesn't love a good story?

Some time back, many years ago, my Soul spoke to me regarding a client and some work we were doing together at the time. He was going through a rough patch at that point in his life and it was affecting his ability to earn an income. He was a day trader at the time and, long story short, we got him back on track, as he was a quick learner. At the time, Bitcoin was trading at about six cents a coin. Yup, that's right. Six cents. Today it is worth around $7,000 a coin, and has had its higher moments.

My client comes to me one day after we had been watching this new coin and says, "Give me $200 and I will put it in for you." He tells me, "I have a hunch, there's something about it," he says. "I can't put my finger on it, but it feels right."

Don't you know, I felt it too, **but** – and there it is, the **But** – I had a lot going on then and was **not willing** to make the effort to **get clear,** to **stay present,** to make a **beneficial decision.** So I politely made an **excuse** and declined. I put this in bold so you can see the pattern that I and many individuals have throughout our lives, of living asleep within the dream.

And so with every decision/choice there is a blessing, or a consequence, or if you wish to call it this, an energy. For every action there is an equal and opposing other action, aka reaction. That is energy, it is always moving.

Remember this next statement for later. Even though I didn't have the courage to accept the gift from my Soul back then, my Soul, my I Am, still saw, and still sees me here and now, as abundant, wealthy and healthy. I could not see myself that way back then, but it could. My Soul knows me and my value. It always did, and always will. Of course I am writing this from hindsight 17 years later, hoping you see where this is going and get the point, as at one point Bitcoin was trading at close to $20,000 per coin – and, well, I will let you do the math.

That said, this is the same for a serious health issue. Your Soul knows your divine blueprint. It sees you as whole, healthy and complete, and it can help you to return to that place. If you're willing to go in thought to that place and time when you went off track – in other words, used your will to go astray from the easiest track in your plan – your Soul can and will help. All you have to do is **ask sincerely**. I mean, you have to really mean it, and it will know, don't you worry.

Why am I telling you this? No, it's not so you can have a good laugh (or cry) at my expense, but you probably are. That's OK. Now get up off the floor and listen to the story I am going to share.

When I moved to Santa Barbara, California I did so on a hunch, a feeling, a gut instinct if you will. You know the one, when your Soul speaks to you almost out loud. Suffice it to say that finances were lean before starting the journey, as I stated earlier. Then with the disasters here in Santa Barbara and my skewed perspective on life, well, things just got really crazy financially.

Shortly after the mudslide in January, a close friend who is an investor type and a brilliant woman who knew my situation, said, "I think you should look into this particular investment." Now here's me: "You know my situation, why would you present this to me now?" Really, is this happening again, 17 years later? Of course I said this to myself. She sensed my apprehension, but realistically it was more like it scared the heck out of me and made me angry. She showed me the payoff if I went for it. Whaaaaaaat! Craaaaazy!

So I pouted a bit, went home and sat on it, as I was still in that head space of lack. Here I was again, in an opportunity to benefit myself, and I was like, I can't pull the trigger. What the heck is going on? I was sitting on it, only it was not an egg and I'm not a hen, so that won't work. There was action required.

But this time, with this opportunity, I realized that I **did** have a choice. So I applied a new Response-Ability. And so I was able to choose to go for it – however, not in the traditional sense.

She and I had a conversation in regards to what I felt comfortable doing regarding the investment. I had never said yes, I had not committed yet.

The next thing I know, an hour later, I receive a text saying, "You're in." My response again, of course to myself, I was like, "What!!! I did not say yes yet! Oh, man, now I owe her the money! What have I gotten myself into now?"

Everything in me was screaming, "This is scary! Waaaait! I'm not ready!!!" It was like being on the biggest rollercoaster in the world and they just released the brake and you knew there was no turning back. Every story in the book came up for me: shame, blame, guilt, not enough, not good enough, never enough, etc. By the way, all these thoughts were not present moment/now thoughts – I just thought I would point that out. Good of me, right, glad I could help. **The mind/ego loves to use yesterday's fears and tomorrow's worries to make my now decisions. So I decided, NO More, and I mean it.**

At first I was looking at this from an older way of thinking, a perspective of, well, if by chance I possibly fail, it will at least be epic, that's for sure. I just kind of felt into what could be the worst outcome, and sat with it. My ego and I had a long, compassionate conversation, until I was OK with the feeling. This was no small feat, I tell you. And by no means am I saying that this is some right or great way of going about this process. However, I am saying that this is how I Surrendered, using all the things we talked about earlier in the book, and it was highly effective and worked quickly for me.

From there, a funny thing happened. I felt a confidence in myself that I had not known before, like I really feel this is working, I can do this. This allowed me to go to the next space, of real, sincere Surrender.

Then I was thinking, well, if I were dying, how would I play this and/or my last days out? This might sound silly, I know – but in essence I *was* dying, dying to an old way of doing Life, learning to finally just *be*. I was thinking and conversing with my Soul at this point all day, every day, and I still am. I said, well, if we were going out, how would we go? Would we roll over and call it a life?

No way, man! We would ride it out wide open and full throttle. I said, if we are going to be remembered for anything, let it be that – living and loving on life wide open, full throttle. Right then and there, I made a committed choice to my Soul to allow it to be in charge and just trust it. In that new Response-Ability, I was able to accept the life I created, and was creating now. In that new Response-Ability, I was able to find my power, and Allow, and Surrender.

What is the new Response-Ability, you ask? It is to be aware of how I feel in every moment, to make authentic and empowered choices, and then to take action in the world with integrity, doing all of this from a place of embodied connection with, and honoring my Soul.

This means – yes, you guessed it – you really need to be on your aware game and always observing yourself in how you show up in the world, in every moment of life. You can't get lazy on yourself. You are your own, and this world's, most important resource. **On a side note here, the most effective tool in becoming aware of myself, for me, was to Slow Down.**

I noticed that at first, living like this was strange, difficult, and I was a bit critical of myself. Then I became less critical, it became easier, and I began to notice things before they came out of my mouth, and then before I could have a judgment on the observation. When I catch myself now I say to myself, *I see you.* And it will usually go one of two ways.

17

The Compassionate Conversation

WHEN MY EGO gets triggered, I have a compassionate conversation and I tell that aspect of myself, the scared little boy, "That's OK, I accept you thinking that," and I allow it, and surrender to it. I do *not* try to stop it, as that would be futile, and it also would then not be able to pass through me easily and quickly. The resistance would stop it, or at the very least, slow it down.

Or it goes like this. I compassionately whisper to that part of myself, "No more. I am choosing differently. We are choosing differently. I am choosing to trust my Soul and myself. We are choosing to trust ourself, our Soul. We can and will do this."

Sometimes the conversation goes on for a bit, but usually it is a short conversation. How it goes just depends on the feeling I get, and how intense it is, and regarding what issue is at hand. Meditation, hypnotherapy and other modalities are helpful, but you have to be able to have a conscious conversation with your own Self.

This is the key to a new Response-Ability. In real life, when your son punches the other kid on the soccer field in the face and knocks him out, or all hell breaks loose in the boardroom, there is no time to say, hold on, I'll be right back, I need to go meditate or call my therapist, see you in 30 minutes. You need to be comfortable in your own skin, so comfortable with all of you that you can do this on the fly. How do you do this? Compassion, compassion and more compassion for yourself, in observation of you. **Stop and take a deep breath. Slow down**. I never really understood the power in that until now, and of course the daily meditations help, for sure.

[My editor's note: *"Prisco, I wonder if you might have written that a little differently, now that you are becoming more familiar with Kriya meditation and Paramahansa's work."* For you, Nancy, anything. This next statement applies to the paragraph above. *"It isn't that you would need to rush off to meditate for half an hour in the midst of the events of daily life, and/or call your therapist. A regular practice of meditation gets you more in touch with your higher self, your soul, Creator/God, and with Spirit, which is of benefit to you all the time as you go through the events of daily life."* The connection is and always was present, all the time, and now I Am Keenly Aware of it, thanks to my meditation practice. I left this note here in the text, as it was absolutely perfectly and divinely placed and written.]

I struggled with this for a long time, and on occasion I still do. As I said earlier on, this is a process for me, and I suspect it is the same for you, so go easy on yourself. What brings one to that place of surrender to find that compassion for oneself is different for everyone. As I stated earlier, I was in a position in life where fighting what seemed like it might be the possible failure of my lifelong dream seemed futile, to say the least. I looked at it as that nothing else I tried had worked or was working. I had no way that I knew of to raise money to pay the rent, and the little I had saved was gone.

So here, I have another story for you on something else that happened to me that has led to me asking myself more Questions. By now you should be used to me and the stories and questions. If not, you can always use the book for a doorstop or coaster. I hope you get value from my relating this experience, as it was a real eye-opener for me.

There was a point after the fire and mudslide that there was no money left and no money coming in. This was scary, to say the least. I had to at some point fess up to my awesome landlady and tell her that I was not going to be able to pay the rent, and that quite frankly I didn't know when I would be able to. Don't even get me started on all the other expenses, bills and debts. Like I said earlier, after I was able to get myself to **feel** into what could be the worst outcome, along with that came the idea of living out of my SUV. Well somehow I was able to come to that place, and be appreciative and grateful for it, as well as using the techniques I spoke of earlier and which will be reviewed in the last chapter, lest you forget.

That said, in my conversation with my landlady, after I told her all this, the response I received was not the one I'd expected. She just said, "Well, this is going to be tough on us all, and we will work together, let's just see how it goes." She said it as if she was not worried at all, as if she was already prepared for life's little and big contingencies. Right there I saw my dad's face, BAM, and the light bulb went on. She, like him, believed in me, even when I did not believe in myself. So now I had just been called out by life again, and I had to own it, that I was still not trusting myself. A total stranger trusted and believed in me more than I believed in myself.

Right here is where I really had to get honest with myself again and look at why. So I asked myself – how is it that a total stranger, who has only known me for a few months, is trusting me more than I trust my own Self? How is this possible? I began to realize that she could see the real me and my true potential. She did **NOT** see what I saw in me. She was able to see to my Soul essence, what my own Soul saw in me, and decided to trust herself in that. Like I said earlier in the book, my Soul knew and knows my true potential. So I decided to do just that, to trust myself in the way that my Soul trusts me, and **live a life worthy of the calling to which I have been called**. As I meditated on this, I saw this much clearer than I ever had before, and it allowed me to find what I needed within me to trust myself. (This is one among many reasons why it's important to keep good company.)

So I went back to my apartment, got down on one knee and bowed my head, half in exhaustion and the other half in a sigh of relief and reverence that I wouldn't have to worry anymore. I said, in such **sincere gratitude** as if I had been rescued on the high seas in a Class 5 hurricane, "You take it. I surrender to you, my Soul, my I Am. I no longer wish to be in charge. Thank you." I gave the little aspect of myself to the bigger part, and reunited us.

It was quite the emotional moment. I just kind of collapsed into it, and there were many tears shed, mostly in apology for not seeing this sooner, and in gratitude that my own I Am, Soul, Creator had never quit on me, and never would, as it cannot, it is me. As it was me, it is me, and it will always be me.

18

OK, OK, I'm Done, I Promise, Maybe

I REALIZE NOW that this is where most of us fall short. We quit on ourselves, as our religions teach us that we are not good enough right from the start. It's only a matter of time, from that perspective, until people give up on themselves. Now I see that your Soul, your I Am, Creator, *is* you, and you are it, and it never quits or leaves you. It was me who stepped away from it, with my skewed perceptions and beliefs. It never stepped away from me. It never could. It never will.

Sometimes it waits patiently until this life is over and reunites with you on the other side, if you don't learn this lesson this time around. And that's OK, too. But why not learn it now?

Here are some tools that might assist you on your journey. This is sort of a fast track summary. Quite frankly, I am not sure how to say this without it sounding like a judgment, but please do your best to see past that.

Even when you screw up, just Accept, Allow and Surrender to it. It's OK. You can never get it wrong. Really. This is the path of least resistance, and it works very efficiently if you let it, as there is no right or wrong in the eyes of your Soul, only in the eyes of man.

To observe myself, I ask myself, How am I showing up right now, right here? What am I leading with? Am I leading with my needs and/or desires? Those are fine, but have I attached a desperate or despairing energy to it? That desperate energy is a pushing energy. No matter how hard you try to not push away what you want, when you come from that energy, everything and everyone gets pushed away.

My mind, my ego, the little voice, whatever you call it – you know the one – has a need to be compassionately loved. I now realize that it will desire this daily, forever, and so it deserves my compassionate attention, at the very least. In the beginning it was not going to trust so easily, so all day long I poured out compassion onto it. Now that I understand this, I always will. That is what I promised to do, as it came to me with its fears every day, sometimes all day, and still does.

An important point here is: Keep true to your word to yourself. If you lie to yourself, no one knows but you and your Soul. But your Soul does know. It is not advisable to break a contract with your Soul. A topic for another day, but for now, take it seriously, as your Soul will.

[My editor's note: *Why is it not advisable to break a contract with your soul? What would happen, if you do that? Since nobody knows about it but you and your soul, what's the difference? Since you have brought this up, don't say it is a topic for another day. You can address this with a sentence and answer this question, completing this topic.*]

This topic was addressed briefly in Chapters 9 and 14, but apparently was missed or blocked by her own ego, so I will repeat it for her and all. If you decide, with your free will, to break a contract, or to go back on your word that you gave to your own Soul, you move into a place of unease known as Dis-Grace, aka, out of your Soul's Grace. Not that this is really possible, but it will **feel** like it. There is no disgrace to your Soul. It truly will never judge you. However, your ego will provide an opportunity for you to judge yourself, and you will feel the bad feeling if you pay attention. Maybe you heard it this way: "This is your conscience speaking, is anyone listening? Hello!!!"

There, I hope that was as much fun for you as

it was for me, because as I write this, my Soul is reminding me that I promised it a bike ride today and that I really need to finish this and go for a ride.

OK, back on topic. This process of the new Response-Ability allowed me to go deeper into myself and handle myself and my fears with great love and compassion. This was something I had never tried before. Go figure.

Doing this allowed me to observe myself and my thoughts with less and sometimes no judgment. When I **felt** myself slip into judgment, I **gently drew myself** back to a neutral place of observation. From this place I had less or no opinion or connection to outcome, so I could see the potentials. Then I would observe what I was **feeling**. Depending on the circumstance, person, place or thing that was happening, I would see if I was making a judgment around it. If so, I would look for the need, compassionately asking myself what need was not being met within me, especially if I noticed that my emotions/feelings had a despairing or desperate energy undertone.

My next step was that if there was another in relationship to me and this was not only about myself, I would look for any judgment coming from either of us, towards self or the other, and try to see what needs in either or both of us were not being met. I would look to see what energy was driving the need or needs. I would do this by asking, is there any desperate, despairing or pushing energy underneath the need? How and where do I feel the energy of this need? If there was a desperate, clingy or despairing energy, I would ask myself if I could let that go and be OK. Once I could identify the need in myself and/or another, the next step was to try to meet the need with compassion.

Sometimes this process took a while. When it involves another, especially a close mirror, like a spouse, child or partner, it can be challenging to un-attach, and not take it personally. But this was the process I used over and over, without fail, to allow me to observe myself, and ultimately to embody my Soul more often than not, bringing peace within me. And remember to **slow down. It is not always easy to remember the power of possibilities that lie within every moment** if you're in a rush or feel that you need to be right.

Funny thing, although I was not laughing back then in my life, my Soul always was there, all along. I just **felt** I couldn't get to it, until I allowed it.

Well I know you're dying to know how it all worked out, and I am tempted to not say. The truth is that as I have been writing these last two chapters, I have been realizing that my investment in trusting and believing in myself and my Soul has already borne its fruit.

As you might have guessed, it all worked out. The investment I spoke about in the earlier chapter has shown its results in my life, especially in me investing in myself and remembering who I Am, the embodied Soul in physical form. Let's just say that energy is working for me, as that is my choice. And so it is.

19

The End—
But Only the Beginning
of Our New Story

MOST RECENTLY, and since the completion of this book, the conversations between myself and both my mom and dad have become much more conscious, especially around spiritual matters, and for this, I am truly grateful.

I think that everyone on this planet, especially as they get older, starts to query within themselves as to what the heck this world is all about, why am I here, and how it all works. It's just a bit goofy when it's your parents and you have the answers to their questions. At this point I sit daily in quiet and silent meditation and speak to my Soul, Yeshua, or Jesus if you prefer, as well as Creator.

Right about now you're saying, "Where is this guy going now? I thought he was done." Nope.

Here is where it gets good, and where your Soul and life reward you for all you are, a Divine child of God, Divine Creator, Source, whoever or whatever God is for you.

I am going to strain your memory here, but do you remember when I said how when we're born, I believe we come in fully connected to our Souls and Creator, and that for me, I felt as if things were off. Well, as always, life proves me out. Life shares truths with me every day – in fact, in every moment of every day, if I am aware enough and stay present with it.

That said, as I mentioned earlier in the book, as a child I **felt** I never fit in and that I was not from here, but as a child, I couldn't quite figure it out. I perceived as a child, if you will, with distorted perceptions, due to my taken-on beliefs. However, that **Feeling came from my Soul, trying to get me the message, "Hey, buddy, you're off course here. Wake up! This is only a dream."** Now my perception is quite different, as I am awake within in the dream and I see clearer – however, by no means do I have it all figured out.

So recently in a conversation with my mom she said, "I am hearing to tell you this." With a bit of quizzical apprehension in her voice she went on, "When you were young [as if I am not still young – I just had to put that in, I can't resist], when you were really small, and I'm pretty sure Paul [my brother] was not even born yet, you used to take one of the candles off the table, and then you would go underneath the table and sit there and just talk. I was not sure to who, but I used to try and listen in, and it sounded like you were saying Isa."

Right there, in that moment, I had this flashback to myself in a cave in another life with a light generated from me, speaking with my Soul and God. Immediately following that, I felt within me Yeshua, Jesus, aka *Isa* as he was known in India, tell me it was He with me, and still is, and always will be.

I told my mom this and she said, "I believe it. It certainly sounded like that, to me."

The Whole Key and Point here is that I was not looking outside myself here, or looking for a confirmation or validation from my mom or dad. I was simply having a conversation, and it came to me. A statement so pure, so clear, and it put it all into completion for me, and brought everything full circle.

I put this into the book so you can see that this is for everyone. I am by no means the only person who has had these experiences. I have spoken to hundreds of people that have had similar childhood experiences. They are for all to have. Our Creator, God, with cosmic consciousness and cosmic intelligence, created us all the same and equal. We are **All** filled with equal love, and God, whoever or whatever that is for you, is and always will love you, and you it, even if you have forgotten how.

Your Soul will always give you what you need, if you will open to it. How, you ask? Great question. I'm glad you thought to ask. Just say, "I know you, My Soul. I know you are there. I can't feel you or see you, but I know. Please help me to find you again, to know you again, to feel you again." And then just breathe, and it will come.

Your Soul, God, Creator, will always meet you where you are, it is law. The Law of Grace was and is given to us by the Almighty to use. All we need to do is **Sincerely** turn to it, surrender to it, open to it, and you/me/we, without question, will be met. *Your Soul and God are Always knocking at the door of your life. The question is, will you slow down, stop busying yourself, and open it.*

✳   ✳   ✳

If you have enjoyed this story, please tell someone you know that you think can benefit from it. It's not to sell more books – this creation has a life of its own. I know the pain that I was in for years, both physically and mentally. People cross each other's paths for reasons known only to them and their Souls. Everyone has a past, and seasons in their life that give them choices, choices that yield blessings or otherwise. If I can shed some light on that for anyone, I am grateful.

I sincerely hope that what I have written and expressed here is and always will be helpful to you. You can use this information to redecorate the landscape of your life, as Reverend Larry says, or to make some real changes in how you perceive things. It's your choice. Know that you can never get it wrong, and that life will always give you another chance, as my story has shown time and again.

Love from Me, Always, in All Ways

*　　*　　*

Life Is About My Relationships ... You will never find yourself in a point in time when the subject of relationships is not an active part of your *now* experience, for everything you perceive or notice or know is because of your relationship with someone or something else. Without a comparative experience, you would be unable to perceive or focus any kind of understanding within yourself. Therefore, it is accurate to say that without relationships you could not exist at all.

—*Abraham-Hicks.*

PRISCO PANZA is a spiritual teacher, physical intuitive and healing facilitator. He assists individuals and groups to embody their Soul. He does this through a variety and blend of modalities using passive and active mindfulness, some of which are spoken of here in this book.

Prisco intuitively uses his unique talents, abilities and gifts with individuals, as he is guided for each Soul. Many individuals he has worked with have experienced physical and emotional healing, and have awakened to their true nature and divine relationship with their Soul.

Using his intuitive abilities of seeing, hearing, feeling, and direct knowing, Prisco feels the emotions of others and is able to pinpoint what blocks any heart from opening. As a result, he brings forth extraordinary teachings through both the written and spoken word that assist individuals in healing the body, awakening the Soul, and transforming their reality through the power of love, compassion, humility and wisdom.

---

lifestyleconsultingservice.com   angeleditions.com

631.662.5310   805.699.6332

NOTES

Your thoughts are important. Important to you, important to me, important to the world. Write them when they come, let them flow and give them a voice. Let them know they are heard and you love them and know you are Loved Immensely.